Happy About™ LinkedIn for Recruiting

By Bill Vick
with Des Walsh

foreword by Conrad Taylor,
President & Past Chairman of the
National Association of Personnel Services (NAPS)

*** Includes over $500 of bonus offers
including a free LinkedIn job posting***

21265 Stevens Creek Blvd.
Suite 205
Cupertino, CA 95014

Happy About™ LinkedIn for Recruiting

First Printing, March 2006
ISBN 1-60005-002-6
Place of Publication: Silicon Valley, California, USA

Trademarks

Warning and Disclaimer

Publisher

- Mitchell Levy, http://www.happyabout.info/,
  LinkedIn Profile: https://www.linkedin.com/e/fpf/16739

Executive Editor

- Scott Allen, LinkedIn Profile:
  https://www.linkedin.com/e/fpf/2369

Cover Designer

- Malcolm Turk, http://www.flickerinc.com/

Layout Designer

- Val Swisher, President, Oak Hill Corporation
  http://www.oakhillcorporation.com/

A Message From Happy About™

Thank you for your purchase of this Happy About book. It is available online at http://HappyAbout.info/linkedin4recruiting.php or at other online and physical book stores.

- Please contact us for quantity discounts at sales@happyabout.info
- If you want to be informed by e-mail of upcoming Happy About™ books, please e-mail bookupdate@happyabout.info
- If you want to contribute to upcoming Happy About™ books, please go to http://happyabout.info/contribute/

Happy About helps companies establish thought leadership, increase leads and facilitate customer adoption. We write and publish books for corporations with a positive spin on educational and controversial topics utilizing case studies, testimonials and war stories from those that have "Been There and Done That!". Please contact us by e-mail sales@happyabout.info or phone (001-408-257-3000) if you are:

- A corporation that would like to explore having us create a book for you
- An author that would like to submit a book

Other Happy About books available include:

- Happy About Outsourcing
  http://happyabout.info/outsourcing.php
- Happy About Knowing What to Expect in 2006
  http://happyabout.info/economy.php
- Happy About Website Payments with PayPal
  http://happyabout.info/paypal.php

Other soon-to-be-released Happy About books include:

- Happy About CEO Excellence:
  http://happyabout.info/ceo-excellence.php
- Happy About Joint Venturing:
  http://happyabout.info/jointventuring.php
- Happy About Working After 60:
  http://happyabout.info/working-after-60.php
- Happy About Global Software Test Automation:
  http://happyabout.info/globalswtestautomation.php
- Happy About Open Source:
  http://happyabout.info/opensource.php

Steps necessary to get access to the additional content and special offers

Congratulations on your purchase of "Happy About LinkedIn for Recruiting"

In addition to this Book, you receive access to additional content and special offers. By following the steps below, you obtain access to a password controlled website that gives you access to over 40 interviews and 11 hours of raw content, in addition to other valuable recruiting resources and the following special offers:

- Free job posting on **LinkedIn** - a $95.00 value!
- Free software program, Contact Capture, from **Broadlook Technologies** - a $200.00 value!
- Free one month membership at **Hireability.com** - a $150 value!
- 20% discount on any **eGrabber** product - potential $100 value!

We will add other offers, when appropriate, and will let you know about them.

The site associated with this book is
http://www.linkedin4recruiting.com. When you first get to that site, you will need to register with the following pieces of information[1]:

- E-mail address (we need a valid e-mail address)
- First name, Last name
- Password (this is your desired password, please pick one that you don't mind being transmitted in the clear)
- BookID (please use this ID number: A1100106)

---

[1]. Please note that this site uses cookies to allow you to easily return once you've been registered.

Within 24 hours, you will be e-mailed your authorization to the site.

Once on the site, the navigation is fairly simple. You have access to all the interviews, the bonus page and the additional resources. On the bonus page, you will see instructions on how to take advantage of each of the offers listed above. For **LinkedIn**, there will be a link you can use to add a job posting credit[2]. For **Broadlook Technologies** and **Hireability.com**, you need to fill out and submit a short form, and for **eGrabber**, you need to shop from the link that you are taken to from the bonus page.

We hope you enjoy this book and the additional information and bonus offers. We will be happy to address any questions, issues or concerns you may have. Feel free to use the contact info on the website or in this book. Happy Recruiting with LinkedIn!

---

2. Once you claim your credit you have 30 days to post your job.

Acknowledgements by Bill Vick

This book was first and foremost a work of love and joy. I'm only the messenger for others and in sharing their wisdom I have been forced to re-evaluate my view of networking, recruiting and using LinkedIn.

Many people were involved in making this book possible but I want to thank **Bob Bassman, Anthony Byrne, Des Walsh, Patty Vick** and the **United States Marine Corps.**

The **USMC** for teaching me the values I live by.

Bob Bassman, owner of Management Recruiters of Plano, and the person who taught me what recruiting could be and led the way by example.

Anthony Byrne, trainer extraordinary, a friend and mentor who constantly challenged me to be all I could be.

Des Walsh, for his intelligence, can-do attitude and true partnership in this effort.

Mitchell Levy, and the team at Happy About are a joy to work with and I'm better off for the experience.

My wife **Patty**, for always believing that I could become the person I wanted to be.

"Being ready is not what matters. What matters is winning after you get there."
Lieutenant General Victor H. Krulak, USMC, April 1965.

Acknowledgements by Des Walsh

It has been a privilege to work on this book and I wish to acknowledge in particular the following people:

Suzie Cheel, for her dedicated support and masterful organizing.

Bill Vick, for being a great colleague to work with and a superb explainer of how the recruitment industry works.

Mitchell Levy, a very supportive publisher and open communicator.

Richard Reardon, a valued colleague and my business coach, for his always wise counsel and unwavering support.

Vincent Wright, for inspiring me to make serious use of LinkedIn, and supporting me as moderator of the LinkedIn Bloggers group.

Dave Taylor and **Dennis McDonald**, my co-moderators on LinkedIn Bloggers, who kept the group happy and productive while I concentrated on the book.

contents

Foreword by Conrad Taylor, President & Past Chairman of the National Association of Personnel Services (NAPS)

When asked to write an introduction for this book on LinkedIn, I was challenged since I did not use LinkedIn. Given my respect for Bill Vick and his accomplishments both professionally and for the staffing industry, I decided to explore this tool. I was consumed from the minute I started reviewing this book. I followed the message and the examples of how to get the results that were possible from the beginning to the end. I am anxious to listen to each interview conducted. I started with 48 direct contacts and now have access to over 506,800 professionals through those initial contacts. To say I have been WOWed would be an understatement. This book is a gold mine of tips and information.

In my career in the US Navy (where I was a Master Chief, Warrant officer and Mustang Lieutenant), I learned that it was important to be good at what you do, but more importantly to have key contacts within every area you interfaced with. No matter what I needed to accomplish, someone in my network "knew a guy that could make it happen".

In my Staffing Industry career, I have certainly used the basic concept I practiced in my Navy career and have tracked the use of technology to automate all the processes that lead to success. I remember introducing Bill Vick in 1994 to a large audience at a NAPS national meeting where only three hands went up when Bill asked who had any automation in their office. From there, Recruiters on Line and a number of other automation systems have become the foundation of tools used to be effective in our industry.

I spent one weekend reading this book, joining LinkedIn and putting into practical use the examples that the interviewees in this book provided. What a tremendous example of shared value. If you did nothing more that read this book, you will receive value! But, I submit that you cannot stop there! 90,000 plus recruiters are not wasting their time by being actively involved with LinkedIn.

LinkedIn can help you on many levels protect your investment in this industry.

You can be sure that in my role as President of the National Association of Personnel Services (NAPS) I will be recommending our members to get LinkedIn and to read and listen to this book.

Conrad G. Taylor, CPC/CTS
President
Past Chairman
NAPS
Conrad.taylor@recruitinglife.com

1 Challenges and Opportunities

Although the online business network LinkedIn was not designed specifically for the recruiting industry, it has become a favorite tool of recruiters. This book, based on many interviews with recruiters who have learned how to leverage LinkedIn's capabilities, shows why.

Like so much else in our era, the recruiting industry is changing rapidly; sometimes it seems to change on a daily basis. At the same time, there are aspects of the business which stay constant and procedures and practices which are effectively timeless.

The basic driver of change in the recruiting industry, as in industries across the spectrum, is technology; specifically, Internet technology. And what makes so many procedures and practices timeless is that, *no matter how smart and fast the technology becomes, recruiting, by definition, is and always will be a people business – about people, by people, for people.*

While there is state-of-the-art technology to support the recruiting industry, the core challenge for any recruiter in this first decade of the twenty-first century is the same core challenge a recruiter has always faced: to find the most placeable candidate for a nominated position and to ensure that particular candidate is selected and hired, whether working on a contingency or retainer basis.

To meet that challenge successfully, the recruiter is required to manage some specific challenges, whether solely or in collaboration with others:

- find jobs and businesses with jobs to offer (hiring authorities)
- research the available field of candidates
- present the most placeable candidates to the hiring authorities
- control the process step-by-step
- repeat the process

Ron Bates,
Managing Principal,
Executive Advantage Group, and the top LinkedIn member in terms of number of connections

"Ultimately what a recruiter is being paid for is to do the best possible job covering a viable candidate population and from that put the best possible candidates in front of their clients."

In addition, on the broader business development front, the recruiter will need to meet the following challenges:

- planning and conducting marketing
- developing and maintaining databases and systems
- finding and collaborating with other recruiters
- establishing and maintaining business continuity

Technology helps recruiters with each of these challenges, turning them into opportunities. Well used, technology enhances effectiveness without replacing the time-tested people-focused processes such as picking up the phone and making a call. For all the capabilities of Internet technology and sophisticated databases, the telephone is often the shortest distance between two points! But technology, and specifically the Internet and World Wide Web, have made the processes much faster and more efficient, to a degree probably unthinkable by most people twenty and more years ago.

The increase in speed is very significant. For example, because many of the processes of recruitment can be carried out more rapidly, recruiters can now bill at higher volumes relative to the time they spend on tasks.

By the same token, hiring authorities have always wanted positions filled promptly and technology has given them heightened expectations of satisfaction. Thus, while the technology provides the recruiter with ways to streamline and speed up the process, there is increased pressure on the recruiter to deliver sooner—and from a more widely and deeply searchable population.

Gerry Crispin,
Principal,
CareerXroads,
and pioneer in
using the Internet
for recruiting

"Technology has improved the efficiency and productivity of the recruiter and the employer."

One particular challenge the new technology represents for recruiters is that it enables client companies to do for themselves much of what they have previously engaged third-party recruiters to do. This threat to recruiters is more likely to affect those whose focus is on the middle range of positions—those which pay between about $50,000 and $100,000 annually.

Also, all recruiters have access to the new search, matching and applicant-tracking database technology, so that objectively, all recruiters are on the same footing when it comes to technology.

The operative word is objectively. We know that even though a whole industry or group of people can face the same challenges, not everyone finds or takes up the available ways, including technology, to deal with those challenges. LinkedIn is a case in point.

There are many online resources and tools. Increasingly, recruiters are coming to see LinkedIn as the premier online tool for recruiters. This is borne out by the interviews conducted for *Happy About LinkedIn for Recruiting*. From these interviews with recruiters, including some big billing industry leaders, it is evident that LinkedIn is the leading online tool to facilitate and enhance a twenty-first century recruiter's success.

On the other hand, it is also evident from the interviews that:

- some recruiters do not see how LinkedIn can help them
- some recruiters who are LinkedIn members do not make full use of its features

Joe Pelayo,
Executive Recruiter;
Chief Executive Officer, Joseph Michaels Inc., and Pinnacle member

"LinkedIn is a breakthrough tool that most people don't understand."

For LinkedIn, that lack of understanding or utilization is a significant challenge. But for recruiters who find out what LinkedIn has to offer and decide to "seize the day" it represents an unparalleled opportunity to dramatically enhance their business. This book shows how recruiters are doing this right now.

Some key reasons for lack of understanding or underutilization of LinkedIn are:

- seeing LinkedIn too simply, as just another database of candidates
- not investigating or utilizing the advanced features of LinkedIn

Arthur Young, *founder at* **Delta Resources International, Recruiter.com and the Recruitment Consulting Group**

Industry specialist Arthur Young, founder at Delta Resources International, Recruiter.com and the Recruitment Consulting Group, commented on the impressive achievement of LinkedIn, in bringing together so many people from the recruiting industry. Speaking of numbers of people in the industry, in North America, he said "If we include staffing and we include the staff at the retained companies, as well as third party recruiters, we're probably looking at about 100,000 people. That would also include contract recruiters who operate on a company site, or using company resources, corporate resources, but are not employees." Add to that an estimated 30,000 recruiters in other countries and it is immediately evident that the more than 90,000 recruiters who are LinkedIn members constitute a very high proportion of the global recruitment industry's population.

It is quite natural that when recruiters first come into contact with LinkedIn, one of the first things to strike them is that with over 4 million members, largely in the executive and professional sectors, LinkedIn is a great source of candidates for a wide range of positions, especially the higher paying ones. And they are not wrong.

There is no question that LinkedIn represents a formidable database of potential candidates. Often many of them are the hard-to-find passive candidates that so much of the recruiting effort is designed to uncover. LinkedIn also represents an incomparable network of people, business owners, vice presidents and others in key positions to decide or influence hiring decisions across a range of industry sectors and many companies.

Craig Silverman,
Executive Vice President of Sales and Marketing,
HireAbility

"What I've learned since becoming an avid user of the application is that it aids a large number of recruitment functions and services. LinkedIn has been a great way for our recruiters to locate some new business opportunities and build relationships with hiring managers that want to take advantage of recruitment services. At the same time, it's a great way for people to find candidates that might be either passively or actively looking for work."

But LinkedIn is much more than a database of potential candidates and hiring authorities. As the interviews conducted for this book have consistently confirmed, LinkedIn has great value beyond its role as a database. In fact, for many very successful recruiters, LinkedIn's value as a networking and marketing tool is seen as being, if anything, greater than its value as a database.

Gerry Crispin

"LinkedIn is a tool for building relationships to contribute to long-term business."

What has also emerged from the interviews is that LinkedIn enables recruiters to find and connect more effectively with other recruiters interested in working collaboratively. LinkedIn has a significant role to play for recruiters looking for such collaborative deals and "splits," arrangements in which two or more recruiters agree to share the search for candidates and split the fees. Through the introduction and referral system on LinkedIn, the availability of detailed profiles, and the provision of endorsements, recruiters can find other individual recruitment specialists and firms with whom they can establish relationships of trust and broach possible collaborative arrangements. In the past year, some 16 per cent of all recruitment deals industry-wide were splits, and interview responses suggest that this percentage can be expected to grow, especially with the help of LinkedIn.

Another way in which recruiters on LinkedIn leverage their membership is by joining LinkedIn-related groups, either the officially recognized LinkedIn groups or one or more of the various online discussion and mailing list groups.

In short, the recruiter who will stand out and excel in the industry today will be someone who has learned to harness the power of LinkedIn and related groups as a marketing and networking tool as well as a highly valued database and aid to managing the recruitment process.

Shally Steckerl,
Lead Internet Researcher, Microsoft Corporation, and author of *Electronic Recruiting 101,* the definitive guide to online recruiting

"I may not necessarily be the person everybody looks for, but I want to be connected or associated with many of the people everybody else looks for. Because ... being that connector, that node in this network, increases my value as a recruiter. So it's not that I use LinkedIn as a huge database like Monster where I can do a search, pull up a résumé and recruit that person. Typically what I do with LinkedIn is market myself, market the opportunity to network with me, and market my company and what I do."

Chris Forman,
CEO, AIRS

"LinkedIn's a great tool. Learn about it. Use it. It changes a lot. One of the things I love about the team at LinkedIn is that they're innovators. They are a rapid prototyping shop of great ideas. And so every day that tool is new and interesting and valuable. And you know I have to go in and learn how to use it. And our labs team goes and looks at it on a regular basis. We're constantly amazed at the cool things it has from a capability standpoint. So learn, use. Don't discount. Don't say 'I looked at it once,' and not go back to it again. Continue to use it. But again, it's only a tool. It's not a panacea."

The following chapters discuss:

- Why and how high-billing recruiters use LinkedIn as a very effective means to market their services and build their networks
- Why LinkedIn is the smart way to start a search for candidates and often the best tool to complete a search
- How LinkedIn can be used to find and develop new business in a trust-based network
- How using LinkedIn effectively can turn cold calls into warm calls, with door-opening introductions and third-party endorsements.
- How to stand out from the crowd
- How LinkedIn facilitates collaboration and splits
- Practical action steps to leverage membership in LinkedIn

2 The LinkedIn Solution to Professional Recruiting: An Overview

General

Bret Hollander,
*Contingency/
Contract Recruiter*

"LinkedIn has a tremendous amount of resources. I think the biggest problem… from the recruiting perspective is that most people are not utilizing everything LinkedIn has to offer, or don't know how to leverage what's there."

**Marc
Freedman,** *Chief
Executive Officer,*
RazorPop;
*Founder and
Executive Director*
at LinkedInPro and
LinkedIn
University; and
*Executive
Director*, The
DallasBlue
Business Network

"There's a lot of shock…when people first experience LinkedIn. It can be very exciting. It is very complicated. There is a lot going on."

This chapter provides an overview of what users must know and do to get maximum leverage from their LinkedIn membership:

- getting known
- getting connected
- getting endorsements
- using the search and reference tools effectively
- LinkedIn's premium services

Particular attention is paid to the "quality vs. quantity" issue, probably the most commonly debated topic online and offline among serious users of LinkedIn.

Getting Known

The first step in getting known through LinkedIn is to ensure your LinkedIn profile is complete and up to date and it is important to ensure you are listed in the right services category

The importance of a complete, current profile

For a job seeker, a complete, current profile on LinkedIn is clearly an advantage. Recruiters on LinkedIn also recognize the importance of their own profiles being complete and up to date, to support them in finding and building business via LinkedIn. That means making full use of the way the LinkedIn profile format enables members to list what they are looking for, in terms of positions, business opportunities or collaborations.

David Teten, *Online Recruiting Specialist, Chief Executive Officer,* Nitron Advisers; *Chairman,* Teten Recruiting; co-author, *The Virtual Handshake: Opening Doors and Closing Deals Online*

"At Nitron Advisors, we focus on leveraging people's virtual presence, via online networks, LinkedIn, blogs, social network sites, virtual communities, and so on. It is more and more normative that people have a virtual presence. Particularly in the tech industry, it's almost standard that before you meet with someone you Google™ them, search for their digital trail. And even people not in the technology industry almost always have a digital trail."

David Allen, *President,* Century Associates and 35-year veteran recruiter

"I think that if you can list the kinds of work that you've done on your profile, you build up your own individual network, and you respond to those individuals on your network to let them know of your specialties and your successes, that enables individuals to be comfortable with you, which in turn makes them feel more comfortable in giving you assignments and in giving you searches to work on."

Shally Steckerl

"Put every job you've ever had on your profile, everything going back all the way to when you were flipping hamburgers at McDonalds, because every one of those experiences can yield other opportunities."

Jim Stroud, *Senior Internet Researcher,* Microsoft Corporation

"I would tell recruiters to optimize their profile. That's paramount. Then I would tell them to list very conclusively what they have to offer, and then list what they are in need of. People want to help people. But you have to help them help you. So listing what you have to give and what you're in need of helps both parties."

Suzanne Tonini,
Chief Information Officer/Sourcer and Research Specialist, *Founder* of MTR Inc.

"List your strengths and accomplishments. And use keywords. Keywords are important anywhere on the Internet. As many keywords as apply to your industry, background, accomplishments, whatever you've done—put them in there. Then anybody who wants to network with you will be able to find you easier."

On the LinkedIn website, under **Listing Your Services on LinkedIn**, there is a good introduction to setting up a profile.[3]

Endorsements demonstrate respect and trustworthiness

LinkedIn's unique endorsement feature is highly valued by recruiters and sourcing specialists.

Shally Steckerl

"Get a lot of endorsements from people you trust. Not fake endorsements, not just asking anybody that you know...Go out there and develop stronger relationships with the people you already know and have them put their name on your page."

Tina Boone,
Recruitment Director, S. J. Gallina & Co. LLP

"I've leveraged LinkedIn into a marketing tool for myself: the endorsements and my statement there, my profile, are very important. I guide my candidates to it. I will send my LinkedIn link to candidates. They can take a look at my endorsements. It helps me build a level of trust with them....I think the endorsements are huge."

---

3. https://www.linkedin.com/static?key=about_providing_services

Join LinkedIn Groups

A number of recruiters make use of groups within the official LinkedIn for Groups category, such as groups for college alumni, professional organizations and industry conference groups.[4] One advantage of being a member of one or more of these groups is the extra search functionality provided within the respective groups.

There are also LinkedIn related groups on other systems, such as the many LinkedIn-related groups on Yahoo!® Groups [5]. These groups, which are set up as forums or discussion groups with mailing lists, provide a way of comparing notes on how best to leverage LinkedIn.

The subject of using groups is discussed further in Chapter 6 in the context of networking.

---

4. There is a directory of these officially recognized LinkedIn groups at
   https://www.LinkedIn.com/static?key=groups_directory
5. See http://www.yahoogroups.com.

Getting Connected

LinkedIn provides some very helpful tools for quickly building a LinkedIn network, based on people the member knows and trusts. One such tool is the Outlook Toolbar which automates the process of collecting the member's existing email contacts, checking whether they are on LinkedIn and then enabling the member to invite them to join the member's LinkedIn network. There is also a provision for importing contacts from other popular personal contacts managers.

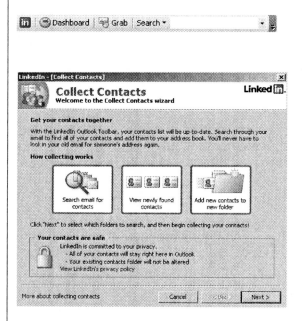

Stuart Thompson, *Recruiting Manager,* **Take-Two Interactive Software, Inc.**

"The Outlook Toolbar is a great timesaver. Any time I can consolidate the amount of things I have open on my computer and be able to use one system to do more than one thing, I'm thrilled about it. I've really found the Outlook tool has consolidated all of the really essential pieces of LinkedIn I really like, such as the searches, and being able to collect and find peoples' information. Giving it to me on a small toolbar has been really beneficial."

TIP For new LinkedIn Users—Personalize the standard or boilerplate LinkedIn invitation messages. This will significantly increase chances of a positive response rate.

Quality vs. Quantity

A regular topic of discussion in various newsgroups, online and privately, is the concept of a "quality" network versus a "quantity" network:

- "quality" in the sense of a small, tight network of people one can work with, know and trust, or
- "quantity" as in a lot of people, who can provide a great deal of access

LinkedIn is understandably very protective of the quality of the network, and this view is expressed in a conservative view of how people should "connect," using the word in the LinkedIn sense of someone actually joining a network and being a first-degree connection, not in the broader sense of "making contact."

LinkedIn management's approach is indicated by the text that a member sees when he or she is about to reply to a request for a connection:

LinkedIn Management

"We recommend that you only connect with professionals you know well and who you are generally willing to recommend to your other business contacts."

Commenting on LinkedIn's rules for connecting, Konstantin Guericke, VP Marketing and Co-Founder at LinkedIn, observed that this issue needs to be looked at on two levels, a basic level of what members are allowed to do in connecting with other members and a level of best practice for networking, which allows for a variety of approaches.

Konstantin Guericke,
VP Marketing and Co-Founder at LinkedIn

"The first level is what is allowed by the user agreement, because those are the rules that everybody needs to adhere to when they're joining LinkedIn. That means that when you invite people, those people already know you. It means that when you contact people, you use the contact mechanisms provided by LinkedIn."

The interviews for this book indicate that recruiters who use LinkedIn on a daily basis have generally been focused on building a large network.

Jon Williamson,
Recruiter,
Williamson Employment

"As I understand it, there are two schools of philosophy on online networking. One is what LinkedIn suggests that you do, which is to connect only with people who you know and trust very well. The other is that you should be open to connection with almost anybody, because you don't know if some gentleman or lady in Belarus may not be acquainted with a software developer in Topeka, Kansas, who knows a hiring manager in Chicago, who may offer you a job."

Marc Freedman

"A recruiter's objective is to get business. It's to generate leads, it's to be known and it's to reach people. So in that context, because that's your business objective, I've seen it work very successfully. And I highly recommend that active, aggressive recruiters focus on building their connections, because once they've built a large list of connections it works multiple ways for them.

"It will allow a recruiter to reach candidates that you didn't have access to and it will bring those candidates closer than otherwise. Instead of being three connections away maybe they're only one connection away."

Peter Weddle,
Owner,
WEDDLE's LLC

"Networking is about relationships. It's about building trust and confidence and familiarity. And you can't do that simply with an e-mail message that invites somebody to come into a network. It has to be developed and worked, in my opinion.

"The feedback that I'm getting is that a message from someone who is not known by somebody else, which comes in through networking technology, is viewed as intrusive. In fact, at a summit that Yahoo!® held last week such messages were actually described as spam – the new spam on the Internet. So I would argue that the quantity idea really does nothing more than facilitate access to the low-hanging fruit, the people who are already likely to move. If they aren't active job seekers they are just about ready to be active.

"If you're trying to connect with the truly great talent, the best talent, the people whose employers already take good care of them, who are highly valued in their field, who make an extraordinary contribution to their employer, then that kind of contact requires a qualitative dimension that I think can be facilitated by the Internet but can't be replaced with a broad, 'shotgun' approach to networking."

Others interviewed for this book emphasize quality, although not to the exclusion of quantity.

Stuart Thompson

"You want to be selective on whom you bring in to your connections and who you have on your list, that they're people that add value to yourself and to what you're looking to do with LinkedIn. And I would encourage people to be selective on bringing in people that you can help and will be able to help you, so that you really create those networking relationships, create mutually beneficial relationships."

Gerry Crispin

"I am not into a quantity model and this is the guy who has 700 people connected to him on LinkedIn and who also believes that I can network with more than 25,000 people in recruiting every month. So when I say I am not into quantity I mean that a bit tongue in cheek. But the point is I'm not focused on quantity, I'm focused on a quality relationship with another individual, a very specific one.

"I will not engage as a connection anyone that I haven't met, and 'meeting with someone' means having a conversation with them after a conference meeting, it means talking to them on the phone, it means engaging them in any number of different ways. I want to have some sense of who this person is and what they're about, and I want them to have some sense of me. So, if that's true and they opt in to a connection with me, that's great."

Craig Silverman

"At HireAbility we encourage people to go in the quality direction because the belief is strong that a good relationship is going to be much more valuable to you. But at the same time, it's almost like a startup company. You need revenue. You need some activity. And with LinkedIn there's some of that quantity activity there as well.

"So, for example, I have a newsletter. 25,000 people read the newsletter that we put out every month. So when I see high volumes of people who read that newsletter and click through, it's very easy for me to see who those people are and potentially invite some of those people and see if they could be interested in being in my LinkedIn network."

A balancing act? What seems to be at issue here is that there are two different perspectives on how best to network. The "quality" argument is for building a strong network by establishing connections with people one knows professionally or personally and with whom there is mutual trust. The "quantity" argument, at least as many recruiters see it, is for building a large network because one does not know at the outset what connections will be needed in the future.

Among the recruiters who use LinkedIn as a key part of their business, the current consensus seems to be that by building a large network as quickly as possible they will have a greater pool of contacts to network with, be they candidates, clients or other recruiters.

It is worth noting however, as Konstantin Guericke pointed out, that with the Business or Pro membership system, searching on LinkedIn is no longer limited to people in an individual's own network, so even recruiters with few connections can now access the entire LinkedIn network.

Konstantin Guericke

"It's really a trade-off that recruiters make between time and money. Some recruiters have a lot more time available than money. They focus on things they can do for free within their own network. For people where time is more at a premium, they tend to go with a Pro account."

Basically, recruiters building their networks need a strategy that works for everyone they deal with, and each of those people will be in one of the following five groups:

- a current or potential candidate
- a current or potential client
- a current or potential reference
- a current or potential center of influence
- a current or potential recruiter for split activity.

There is no doubt that everyone wants quality connections. But recruiters also need to have a lot of connections, including both those currently needed connections and potential future connections, for their businesses to develop and grow. They need to "dig the well before they are thirsty."

None of the interviewees argued for "quantity at any price," but there is little doubt that the more determined recruiters on LinkedIn are keen to have large networks as well as quality relationships.

Using the Search and Reference Tools Effectively

Several recruiters emphasize the importance of using the powerful search capacity built into LinkedIn.[6]

Ron Bates pointed out that as a searchable database, LinkedIn provides an excellent resource with information about millions of people, albeit limited by how much somebody chose to put in his or her profile.

As LinkedIn is an opt-in database, with members having complete control over the content of their profiles and also being able to indicate the types of requests they are open to receiving, people are more likely to respond to requests than if their contact details have been found from some other database.

Speaking of LinkedIn's comparative effectiveness as an organized database, Shally Steckerl used the image of an offline library and, in a dramatic image, likened other search engines to a library card index system, but with the library cards strewn on the floor:

---

6. There is a useful guide to the various search possibilities at the LinkedIn website under Special Search Types:
   https://www.linkedin.com/static?key=pop_more_search

Shally Steckerl

"A lot of times the privileges of membership in LinkedIn allow you access to information that wouldn't normally be publicly available. In other words, it's not part of that card catalog on the floor, it's actually part of one of the books you have to take out of the library and open. But because of that it's much more organized."

Maureen Sharib,
Human Resources Researcher;
Names Sourcer/Sourcing Methods Trainer;
Names Generator at techtrak.com

"I think sourcers are using LinkedIn in the same way as they are using other information portals. They're going to LinkedIn in order to get a 'toehold'."

More than one power user of LinkedIn remarked on its value for finding people in strongly specialized positions, who may be "deep down" in a company and not readily located. Keith Halperin was looking for a RF engineer in Denver and had used other search tools without success. He drilled down in LinkedIn and found someone.

Ron Bates demonstrated how to use the search feature of LinkedIn to connect with an individual the recruiter is not yet acquainted with. His approach is to use LinkedIn to identify relevant companies to generate a peer level search, find people who would know the individual the recruiter is seeking to contact, and then network through those people to connect with that individual.

David Perry,
Managing Partner,
Perry-Martel
International Inc.

"LinkedIn is a great tool! Whenever you search, the hardest part is, you know, starting. Where do you find them? Who are the people you need to talk to? LinkedIn is a great tool for primary sourcing. It's a great tool for trying to break into a company to find out who to talk to, because even if the perfect prospect is not directly in LinkedIn, one of their co-workers probably is."

Some of the search features of LinkedIn may not be immediately evident to a new user but can accelerate a search considerably. For example, a search for a particular person can be done by clicking on the Find People tab, and then clicking on the nested "By Name" tab.

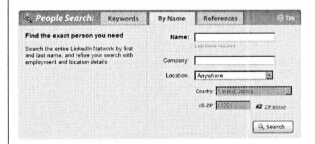

The capacity to search for references is another valued tool for a recruiter or sourcer. It can save a great deal of time in locating people who may know the person a member is interested in contacting, whether as a prospective candidate or for business development. Any member can search for people who have worked at particular companies during specified periods. A member with a Business or Pro account can then check on the most appropriate way to contact the individuals concerned.

One-Click Reference Business or Pro account holders have access to the powerful one click reference tool, which is linked to each of the profiles displayed in the reference search results. This tool allows you to quickly see who in their network may have worked with the person in question, and refine the search progressively.

Ronda Woodcox, *Owner and President,* Talent Scout Recruiting

"I was conducting a search for a Fortune 100 company, where I'd used the connections and referrals approach on LinkedIn. One of the people contacted me back and said 'I'm not qualified for this. However, I do have a group that I'm involved with, that I run, and I would very much like to be able to post your information about this position.' At that time, none of these people were involved with LinkedIn and I was able, through this contact, to tap into this amazing resource of people who were incredibly qualified and exactly what my client was looking for. From there, I was able to place them and it worked out very successfully. I never would have known of that person without LinkedIn."

LinkedIn's Premium Services

The premium account system on LinkedIn is relatively new, but there is no question that the search capability is significantly enhanced by upgrading to a premium account. Any of the premium accounts provide expanded profiles for candidates outside the member's own network. According to LinkedIn, the typical user has fewer than 80 connections and a network of fewer than 30,000, so upgrading to a premium account has a dramatic multiplier effect on the member's reach, because it provides access to the whole, 4 million plus network. The premium member is also able to contact any of these members directly.

The table below shows how a Business, Business Plus or Pro account gives much more access to the LinkedIn network than a Personal (free) account. These premium accounts also provide access to LinkedIn's InMail service and render the member more accessible (in a personally controllable way) to other LinkedIn members, through the ✿ OpenLink system. They also allow the member to send more invitations and InMails, the numbers increasing with the level of premium account, from three a month for a Business account to fifty a month for a Pro account. There is also a response guarantee: if a candidate doesn't respond within seven days, premium account holders automatically get a free InMail credit to contact another candidate directly.

Compare Account Types

	Personal Free	Business	Business plus	Pro
		Upgrade	**Upgrade**	**Upgrade**
Receive Introductions	✓	✓	✓	✓
Send Introductions	✓ 5 at a time	✓ 15 at a time	✓ 25 at a time	✓ 40 at a time
Receive InMails	✓	✓	✓	✓
Send InMails		✓ 3 per month	✓ 10 per month	✓ 50 per month
Receive OpenLink Messages		✓	✓	✓
Reach over 4.4 million users		✓	✓	✓
Unlimited reference searches		✓	✓	✓
More LinkedIn Network results		✓ 100	✓ 100	✓ 200
Expanded LinkedIn Network profile views		✓	✓	✓
OpenLink Network membership		✓	✓	✓
Upcoming feature sneak peeks		✓	✓	✓
Priority customer service			✓ 1 business day	✓ 1 business day

Learn more about Business and Pro account benefits.
Please contact us to learn about more account offerings.

[1] Maximum number of pending introductions

Randy Bogue,
Managing Director,
Venator Partners

"We use InMail frequently. We find that we're pleased with the value we receive from it. And we use it on pretty much every search. It's not exclusively what we use, but we use it."

Another premium service, tailor made for recruiters with multiple positions to fill, provides for:

- Purchasing 'job packs' in multiples of five or ten
- Arranging directly with LinkedIn to advertise jobs on the basis of a corporate subscription.[7]

Because responses to the job advertisements come through the LinkedIn system, the recruiter who is advertising is able to see any connections the applicant shares with them and whether any of the recruiter's connections has worked with the applicant at some stage.

Recruiters using this service can also let their own network know about advertised positions, which could result in a passive candidate being attracted to apply.

---

7. See http://www.linkedin.com/hiring.

Roger King,
CEO, **Chief People Officer**

"We started out with InMail when InMail first came out and we really see the value of InMail, in that it gives us the opportunity to contact people directly, rather than going through the chain of our two to three referrals that might be between us and the person that we're trying to get to.

"I think we go through 50 to 100 InMails a month. I think the success rate's pretty high. On the one hand we're pretty conservative on how we use InMails, because we want to keep out five star rating, meaning we make sure the InMails we send out are appropriate to the profiles of the candidates we're posting to. So we're not doing large InMail blasts. And I would say the response we've had has been probably 80% 'Yes, I'm interested' and 20% 'No, but thank you'.

"The response is high because (a) you can read the profiles of the candidates, whether or not they're open to a career opportunity, and (b) you can read something about their background and what they're doing and get a feel for whether they are or might be a fit for your current client."

Checklist for Action

- ☐ Become known on LinkedIn
- ☐ Have an up-to-date profile
- ☐ Seek quality endorsements
- ☐ Join LinkedIn Groups
- ☐ Get connected building a large network based on quality connections
- ☐ Use search and reference tools effectively
- ☐ Upgrade to a Premium account

3 LinkedIn for Marketing and Finding New Clients

LinkedIn, with its four million-plus members and a powerful search engine, is obviously a potential tool for recruiters seeking candidates for various positions. The bigger picture, which is not always obvious at first glance, but clear to expert recruiters who are experienced LinkedIn users, is this: LinkedIn is a powerful networking tool, with significant benefits for recruiters marketing their own services, finding opportunities for business development, and locating candidates.

Vincent Wright,
Founder and
President, Wright
Enterprises

"I think LinkedIn's strength shows up in finding clients. It gives you a huge, almost inexhaustible array of companies and executives you can read about in unusual detail. You have their profiles there, in most instances. You have an opportunity to see who they know as well. So it gives you a rich pool of knowledge."

The importance of a complete, current profile

As several quotes in the previous chapter showed, a number of people interviewed stressed the importance of the LinkedIn profile for marketing and attracting new business. Having a well-constructed, up-to-date LinkedIn profile is clearly an essential step for a LinkedIn member seeking to be hired. Individual recruiters should also ensure that their profiles communicate their own messages to the market as comprehensively and with as much detail as possible.

Shally Steckerl says a profile that works for LinkedIn networking will be different from a "résumé-style" profile, where most people put in what they think are the highlights of their careers. He recommends having a profile that tells your story: what you are like and what makes you who you are, and to put every job you have ever had on your profile, using as an example his own profile's reference to having been in the Peace Corps as "one more way I can connect."

But a good profile needs more than an interesting story. An effective profile in LinkedIn's elaborately constructed, highly searchable database system will incorporate the key words for the LinkedIn member's interests, employment history and industry, even casual or vacation jobs. It will also include accurate titles, as this is a specific, well-used field for LinkedIn searches.

Case Study: Improving the Value of Travel by Connecting with Prospective Clients

The geographic search capability of LinkedIn is very helpful when recruiters are looking for prospective clients in specific locations.

Carl Kutsmode,
Human Capital Management Consultant,
Expertise in Recruitment Process Optimization and Outsourcing

"About a year ago I was traveling to the Pacific Northwest. I only had one client meeting set up in Seattle, didn't have any other prospects out there. I thought, well, let's see who's in LinkedIn connected to me and what companies are out there. Sure enough, through a LinkedIn connection, I got a connection at Expedia.com. Didn't end up doing business yet, but got a meeting and some great insights into the organization. I'm staying in touch with them and have actually gotten referrals to candidates from that person."

Rick Shull, Executive Search Consultant, also uses the geographic area search capability of LinkedIn to look for potential new clients in areas where his firm does business:

Rick Shull,
Executive Search Consultant

"I have utilized LinkedIn from a marketing perspective. Oftentimes, what I will do is I look for members of LinkedIn that are in the geographical areas in which we do business and oftentimes will reach out to them through LinkedIn to see if they would be open to what you might call 'meet and greet' sessions, to introduce our services, and to hear more about what they do. That's been somewhat effective, especially in the geographical markets where our firm is known."

Gerry Crispin talked about how a small recruiting business can better utilize LinkedIn to find new clients:

Gerry Crispin

"I would be focusing in on clients, and looking at identifying potential clients, using LinkedIn, and would stay away from multi-national firms. I would be focusing on firms where I can have an introduction and would work my way down a chain that allowed me to engage small firms about their interests, their needs and what gaps I might be able to fill."

Gerry also spoke about how he uses LinkedIn as part of his marketing:

Gerry Crispin

"So number one, I think it's part of my sales and marketing strategy. My interest in using LinkedIn and a couple of other services, is in connecting or meeting every person that influences staffing in a major corporation in the United States. So that's a finite number of companies, that's a finite number of people. I know the names and the titles of everybody in this country that I want to meet and I know what percentage of them I've already met.

"My accessed information on LinkedIn gives me a list of companies, the people in them and their titles and often their contact information, as well as who I know who knows them."

LinkedIn broadens the recruiter's field of possibilities for new business:

Doug Beabout,
professional speaker, training and coaching consultant and contractor

"I think LinkedIn has become widely popular for a very good reason. It provides us with an electronic means to get to know others on all levels, who can help us to do business, where otherwise we would not even be aware. And so it expands our vista. It gives us an opportunity, not only to hook up with people who may use us as recruiters, or may become a placed candidate. But it goes so far beyond that, because it gives me opportunities to meet people in other cultures. It gives me an opportunity to meet people in other venues where I'm not involved directly at my own recruiting desk. And it gives me a chance to understand what's going on somewhere else and what's hot and what's not. I mean, just on a raw level it's a great networking tool."

"But it also leads me towards people who lead me towards people who are clients. And I don't know what that old saying is, but I think we're all, what, seven people removed from everybody else? And LinkedIn cuts that number down considerably. I've had so many interesting people contact me because I put a profile on, I contacted others, I worked the system. And people have contacted me that I had no idea I might be able to do business with and did do business with, simply because LinkedIn was there and it works so well."

David Perry finds new clients by seeking opportunities for candidates who have been short-listed for positions but not hired for those positions:

David Perry

"Every time I find a search I finish up with five or six guys that are great and you're only ever going to have one of them. And if you've done your job right as a recruiter it usually comes down to a 'fit' of chemistry. So the question becomes, what do I do with the other five guys?

"The answer to that question is that I get hold of them and I say, 'You went through the dance and you weren't successful, for whatever reason. Are you interested in continuing the process?' And if they say yes, then I'll log on to LinkedIn and I'll do a search for companies in the same area, either in the same area of industry or the same geographic area, or both. I'll find who the President is and the VP of Engineering, or whoever I happen to need. And I'll go and do a presentation of one or two of those candidates to that employer."

In a comment with special resonance for people with in-house recruitment responsibilities, Kevin Wheeler explained the value to be gained for a company's employment brand by encouraging people well-disposed to the company to join LinkedIn.

Kevin Wheeler,
President/Founder
Global Learning Resources, Inc.

"If you can get people who have a positive view of your company to be in the LinkedIn network and to talk about it in positive ways in their communication with their friends and in any of their social activities, you're promoting the brand. And the more people you have, the more 'friends of the company' you can get into your network, the broader and better your corporate employment brand is going to become."

A Path of Trusted Connections

One of the advantages of LinkedIn for recruiters wanting to connect with potential clients is that LinkedIn provides a path of trusted connections to key people in companies the recruiter would like to engage as clients. The internal LinkedIn e-mail system, InMail™, is also helpful, especially as the recipient knows the sender paid to reach the recipient, unlike regular free email, and the InMail™ Feedback system shows the recipient how the last ten people contacted by this person via InMail responded to those contacts, whether favorably or not.

David Teten

"It's easier to get to people on LinkedIn because there's a path to get to them. One of the reasons why LinkedIn is successful is that, to quote Ross Mayfield[8], 'email is broken'. It's more and more difficult to get people's attention with just an email, because email is so overburdened with spam, bulk cc'ing, and so on. With LinkedIn's InMail™ system, as well as their standard referral system, there is a way to get people's attention much more effectively than with a simple, direct mail."

---

8. Ross Mayfield is CEO and founder of SocialText

Case Study: Building Business by Helping Another with Strategic Introductions

Josh Arnold, *Owner*, Arnold Career Services, a nationwide recruiting service

"I try to find anybody in the recruiting field or people who would have use of recruiters or people who are in our industry, and I respond to different newsgroups.

"These are great opportunities to post, to look at the kinds of challenges recruiters are faced with, those charged with acquiring professional staff, talent, for companies, and it's a great way to interact with people. So the more people you can reach out and help, the better off you are. Let me give you a little story. I received this message from LinkedIn where someone asked me, 'Will you link me up to so-and-so?'

"I got it and I'm reviewing it. The man is an auditor of workers' compensation profiles for companies. So I asked him the question, I wrote back and I said, 'I've made your referral as requested: do you do work for the public sector?' And he wrote back, yes, absolutely. So I wrote and introduced him to the local Mayor, the Deputy Mayor and the Personnel Director of our town, and said, 'This is the service this man provides, this might be something you could use'. Then I wrote to a guy I used to work with, a former colleague, because I was in educational administration. He's now the Executive Director of the Massachusetts Association of School Business Officials. I wrote to him and said, 'Look, this is a good guy, good services, it's a value-added proposition, business officials could use this.' Then at the same time, I wrote to the auditor guy, I cc'd him on the whole thing and said, 'You should write to this guy—join their group as a vendor, there's a price involved, and then get access to the distribution list of the people that are there: that's a great market opportunity.'

"It took me probably three or four minutes out of my day to help that guy but I just opened up multiple, you know hundreds or so doors of business opportunity for him. He's forever grateful. That's where you give something back to the industry, and eventually those things filter out and eventually someone's going to do the same thing for you."

Standing Out From the Crowd

Marc Freedman pointed out that with tens of thousands of recruiters on LinkedIn today, those who want to be successful will need to stand out from the crowd through smarter marketing, including personal or business branding as well as marketing candidates.

Other interviewees emphasized various aspects of marketing that can be enhanced by more effective use of LinkedIn.

Gerry Crispin

"The market part is how you position yourself as a recruiter. That actually helps you three ways: it helps you in terms of people who are running searches and want to find you; it helps you in terms of sending out requests that you want to be accepted; and it helps you in terms of finding candidates.

"Anybody in any business should start with the point of who are these prospects out there and what are they about? Who do they know? Do any of the people I know, know them? Do they show up in various places that I could also go to and meet them?"

Ron Bates

"LinkedIn's an additional branding tool to help brand myself in the firm that I work for from an exposure perspective. You know you've got a profile in there, it can be hit by people that are doing searches, when they are looking for services, for example.

"In terms of reaching out to people, if I identify a company that I think could precipitate either an immediate or a future opportunity, I can obviously identify an executive and then figure out how I want to approach them. Being able to use LinkedIn as a database to identify corporate executives, from a business development perspective is, I think, of huge value."

Jerry Bernhart,
Owner, **Bernhart Associates Executive Search**

"It's natural just to send a message through to somebody saying, 'Hey, I may have a great candidate. Can I contact you? I know about your business. I've checked your website. I've looked at your bio on LinkedIn, so I know something about you and your background and your business, what you do. I may have someone that you may be interested in.' I mean, what a great way to market candidates! Because that's more of a warm marketing contact. It's not calling someone out of the blue."

Checklist for Action

- ☐ Have a well-constructed, up-to-date LinkedIn Profile
- ☐ Develop trusted connections
- ☐ Help others with introductions
- ☐ Stand out from the crowd
- ☐ Check a potential client's profile before making contact (create a warm marketing contact)

Chapter 3: LinkedIn for Marketing and Finding New Clients

LinkedIn for Candidate Sourcing

In using LinkedIn for finding candidates, recruiters need to recognize that they are operating in a climate of intense change. They are facing a boom or bubble, where the aging population will depart from the workforce and there will be an immense talent gap. That coming gap represents many opportunities, both good and bad, for recruiters. The good part is that recruiters will have as much work as they can handle, the bad part is that it will be increasingly difficult to find the right people with the right talents for companies.

Networks like LinkedIn give the recruiter an opportunity to interact and interface with the passive candidate who is not knocking on the recruiter's door, and allows the recruiter to knock on the candidate's door. Because a LinkedIn profile is provided directly by the owner and is completely and directly editable at any time by the profile's owner, it can be expected to be much more accurate than profiles on other databases built by automatically generating profiles based on information from the Web and/or SEC filings. Additionally, many professionals at the Director level or in internal roles (like legal, IT and purchasing) don't show up in press releases or in databases compiled from mentions on the Web, but may maintain their professional profile on LinkedIn.

Roger King,
CEO, Chief People
Officer

"We start the recruiting process by wrapping our arms around what the ideal profile is of the candidate the client's looking for, what type of company they need to come from, the specific industry, the specific role that individuals held in the past and the challenges they might be facing moving forward. So the beginning of our process is basically research, meaning where are those companies, where are those individuals, where do they hang, where do they meet, where do they speak, and of course where they are currently working? LinkedIn is a valuable tool in terms of finding those passive candidates and getting into their network and starting preliminary conversations."

Glenn Gutmacher,
Recruiting Researcher at Microsoft Corporation and *Founder* of Recruiting-online. com

"LinkedIn is the largest portal, in terms of number of professional users, that would be of value to a recruiter. There may be other, larger networks in total, but if you're trying to find the kind of information about potential candidates that a recruiter would need to act on, LinkedIn has the critical mass for that."

Among the various candidate search resources available to recruiters, LinkedIn may in many instances be the most appropriate place to start searching:

Keith Halperin,
Recruiting Lead, Senior Recruiter, Recruiting Strategist, Recruitment Process Outsourcing (RPO) Consultant

"Many LinkedIn people are available through other channels but you're able to find them through LinkedIn first, and more efficiently."

LinkedIn's search options lend themselves to systematic searching for candidates and some lateral thinking about search parameters:[9]

Brian Anderson,
President,
BA Search Group;
Executive Search Consultant

"If I've got a search that I'll conduct I'll get on LinkedIn and populate the keyword search. Or I may use the competitive companies, I may use the academic tie, I may use the geographic tie. But I'll try to go at it with four or five different approaches. I may tap into any associations that person may belong to, whether it's a triple E group or specific category, and then I'll work it four or five different ways. And you know that sometimes you may tap into a contact who may not be an exact fit, but that person's going to guide you to the perfect candidate.

"I kind of use it with the idea that if you're not the target you're still going to be a great opportunity for me to network with."

Vincent Wright described how he would go about conducting a typical search for a candidate, emphasizing his use of Boolean search operators:

Vincent Wright

"Start with what you need: who do you need to have for this particular job? I'd start with a well-constructed argument for what I'm looking for, I'd construct a good, healthy Boolean search string. It really doesn't take that much work to construct those search strings. I'd let the Boolean search strings help me out as much as possible. I'd then go through my searches and I'd look at the results.

---

9. There is a detailed explanation of various search options and functions, including Boolean search operators, at the LinkedIn website, under Special Search Types:
https://www.LinkedIn.com/static?key=pop_more_search#stypes

"What LinkedIn then does, it gives you a table of ten people at a time that you can look at. It also gives you a little snippet about what the person's experience is, and some of the keywords will probably be highlighted there as well.

"I'd review the person's profile as I would normally review a résumé. I'd then click to see who they know. If they make those details available, that could be very, very helpful. And that means you can get additional information from your own contacts who may know the person, who may help you with an introduction."

In speaking about searching for candidates, several recruiters spoke of the need to realize that while LinkedIn might not produce the specific candidate a recruiter wants, it is an excellent resource for narrowing the search for that candidate.

Ron Bates

"LinkedIn's a database that's searchable, like a lot of other databases that you might have at your disposal, either because they're your corporate databases or they're subscription-based. You go in to find people, you make the keyword searches that make sense given what you're trying to do, to narrow it down and identify people that, based on the information you're exposed to, look like they have resonant background for the search you're trying to fill at any particular time, whether you're a recruiter or you're a hiring executive at a company that's trying to fill a position.

"LinkedIn is a great resource, given the fact that it's got over four million people in it. You're somewhat limited by how much information someone chose to put in a profile, so far as how you end up hitting them through searches. But then there's also identifying companies that would precipitate a peer-level candidate for a search that you're doing. If you can't find that candidate in LinkedIn, you might then try and find an individual who would logically know that candidate from a peer perspective that you can then target and network through to get to that individual. It's basically using LinkedIn as a database to identify people and candidates."

Carmen Hudson, *Staffing Manager,* **North America Business Unit, Starbucks Coffee Company**

"LinkedIn is an extremely valuable tool that allows the average corporate or third-party recruiter to work like an executive search consultant. When I was an executive search researcher, we spent hundreds of hours per position doing the legwork to develop a network of appropriate candidates. With LinkedIn, I can create a very targeted network in minutes."

Greg Buechler,
Director of Talent Acquisition,
iHire, Inc.

"LinkedIn is an exceptionally good tool for certain types of research, identifying individuals directly. And that's primarily how I have used it typically. I've used it as a direct sourcing tool."

A candidate search on LinkedIn can be complemented by running an advertisement on LinkedIn Jobs. After an all-day searching session, David Perry had a very positive response from an advertisement:

David Perry

"Very recently I did a project for a product manager. I probably started about 6 in the morning and didn't bring my head up until about 5 o'clock at night, but I ended up with an exhaustive list of people that I wanted to talk to. I probably went through about 1,100 profiles. And LinkedIn had just recently come up with the ability to put an ad on LinkedIn Jobs and I ended up running an ad as well.

"The response to the ad on first day was that I got 9 responses, on the second day I got 37, on the third day 52. I don't remember the fourth or fifth days, but they kept coming in for probably about two weeks. By the middle of the second day, the responses that came in saved me the trouble of having to go after these guys. I'd found three that I was definitely interested in and I folded that down to one within three days. We closed in about two weeks, through the interview process."

LinkedIn Jobs helps you fill your hiring needs:

1 Promote your job to your network and beyond

2 Use LinkedIn's insight to identify the people who come recommended

3 Search your network to find top candidates, references, and more

Several interviewees mentioned the usefulness of LinkedIn for seeking hard-to-find passive candidates for specialized positions.

Sandy Sanderson,
Founding Partner,
Meridian Executive Resources

"I recently completed a CEO search for a hard-to-locate executive, for an early stage company. The usual process would have taken a month, to make many calls and maybe come up with twenty contacts and ten candidates. Running one placement ad on LinkedIn generated qualified candidates, and over seventy-five new contacts. I was able to find five candidates in less than a week and completed the search in three weeks."

Taj Haslani,
Owner and President,
NetPixel Inc.

"LinkedIn is playing a very important role in a very hard-to-find-talent area. We don't use LinkedIn for finding a Java programmer, but we use it for locating people with specific business knowledge and skills in certain areas."

Eric Misch,
Business Development Manager,
Mankuta | Gallagher

"We recently worked on a systems architect position for a software company in the North East and this individual traveled roughly up to fifty percent of his time and definitely was not looking for employment at that time. And we used LinkedIn. We found him on LinkedIn. We contacted him and he's now deep into their interview process. We expect him to be hired. There really wouldn't have been any other way to find this individual. They were located in a different area, a different marketplace and he was not looking for a job at the time. He would not have had any reason to make himself visible."

"We know in today's recruiting world it's getting more and more difficult to find the passive, non job-seeking candidate. LinkedIn's a great way to do that. I'm not sure how long this revolution, so to speak will last, but as long as it does, I think LinkedIn should be used by everyone."

Case Study: Candidate Search Against the Odds, With Bellringer Result

Susan Hand,
Executive and Senior Recruiter,
Getronics

"I had a very hard-to-fill position on the West Coast, in California, in an area I did not know and in an industry I did not know. I was able to search a database," Susan Hand, Executive and Senior Recruiter at Getronics, recalled.

"This was not a job I could post. We didn't exactly have the position yet. I couldn't post the position, I couldn't solicit résumés. I was able to do a search and drill down through some of my sourcing techniques. So I came up with three lead résumés. Two of these résumés were already employed by Getronics and one of the résumés was employed by the chief industry competitor. I contacted that person who turned out to be just two degrees away from me on LinkedIn, and not only was she successful in filling the position, but she was offered a more senior level position and now runs the industry. Also, from that we were afforded an extension of the business contract because our candidate was so full of quality that she hired other qualified candidates around her. So the client, the staffing augmentation client, gave us $10 million in additional business."

In the light of this experience, it's understandable that Susan remarked, "I can't understand why every single recruiter in America isn't on LinkedIn!"

Case Study: Substantial Fees For Two Positions Sourced From LinkedIn

Craig Silverman

"We had a new member come to us about three or four months ago, a small recruitment firm with a very large client, a well-known telecommunications company. They had a very good relationship with the hiring manager, they had a lot of job orders that were active. But these candidates were extremely difficult for this person to locate, so they decided to join the HireAbility network so that our team of 130 plus recruiters could help them to generate candidate flow, in hopes of making split placements. The recruiter who jumped on these orders happens to be an avid user of LinkedIn and she went to work networking through her networks and searching, making requests et cetera through the LinkedIn system, to try and find some people.

"She was very fortunate. There were two jobs that were open at the time. Both of these were very high level positions, salaries north of $200,000, each at a 25 per cent fee. These were very large contingency fees that were involved here and through LinkedIn she found, not one, but two candidates for these two different positions. Both of these positions ended up getting filled through a very lengthy interview process that took a couple of months' time. But in the end she made two placements. The fees that were generated were around $65,000 from these two placements, and in the database and on the placement data form the source for the two candidates was noted as LinkedIn."

Case Study: Using the LinkedIn Tools to Narrow The Search

Bret Hollander, whose company's main focus of candidate searches is for people with high-level security clearances for government positions, described LinkedIn as "a wonderful tool" which he has made extensive use of to make many placements. He provided the following case study to show how he used LinkedIn's search capability in seeking a candidate for a specialist position.

Bret Hollander

"Beyond looking for secret and top-secret candidates I have other clients that know of me and ask me to do work on their behalf, and their requirements have nothing to do with the intel community. Let me give you an example.

"Today I did a search - and you'll see on my profile that I do work with clients who need real-time embedded engineers - so I put in the keyword 'embedded.' Then I did a basic search with just the word 'embedded' in the keywords and it brought up about 500 users. Then I refined the search and said beyond 'embedded' I wanted to focus specifically on the industry pertaining to 'computer hardware'. Of course the list is going to be more refined. That's what you're trying to do, focus on your specific area. So I click on 'computer hardware' as another feature and from 500 I get down to 305.

"And now let's say my employer wants me to focus more on people in his backyard so I choose "located in or near" and I put in his zip code. I search again and I come up with three contacts. Now this might not seem like a lot, but I'm not really looking at LinkedIn from the point of view that this is the person I'm going to solicit for a particular opportunity. The way I'm going to look at LinkedIn is, this is the person I'm going to solicit in terms of who they might know, as in 'birds of a feather flock together', and see if I can network through them to identify more people I need on behalf of the particular company I'm recruiting for."

Case Study: Leveraging LinkedIn's Advanced Search

Joe Pelayo

"Today I'm trying to talk to some Big Four people. I've been retained by a bio-tech company to find someone to run their SEC reporting. They would take someone out of the Big Four accounting firms, so I was expanding my network, going back through LinkedIn. You can search by company names. So I entered 'KPMG' and the other Big Four companies and I entered my area, and then I selected an Advanced Search.

"Whenever you have an option of a regular search or an advanced search, you click on Advanced. Under an Advanced Search you can search by people new to LinkedIn in the last thirty days. So I did that and I added about six names to my search from each of the Big Four."

Case Study: A Quick, Effective Search In An Emerging Technology Space

Candidate search on LinkedIn does not always have to be gruelling or very complex, as David Perry found with a search for a product manager:

David Perry

"I went onto LinkedIn and did a product manager search in the technology space, for VoIP and I put 'VoIP' as a search term. I put the title as 'product management' or 'product manager' and they just popped up. It was that simple."

Joe Pelayo's Hitherto Secret Ingredient for LinkedIn Search: Re-name the Position

"I was retained by a company to do a search for a Director of Revenue Recognition.

"The first thing that I did was to sit down with the company—it's a big software company—and explained to them that that was the most common title for these types of people and we needed to re-work the title a little bit. They said 'What are you thinking? What have you got in mind?' Anyway, we got together and sat down and brainstormed for twenty minutes and came up with a new title, which was a 'Director of Worldwide Revenue Operations'. And I'll tell you we had our pick of the litter, because people would hear that title - the title's your curb appeal, you know. If they don't like the title they're not going to come in and look around."

"The first thing I do on any search is re-work the title. I make it as sexy a title as the company will allow. If it's a manager I want a 'Director,' if it's a Director of Revenue I want something 'Worldwide.' If it's a Controller I'm going to make it a 'Global Controller.' If it's not global I'll make it a 'U.S. Controller'. I want to make it something that's different, that's going to make it stand out from all the other jobs that are out there."

Checklist for Action

- ☐ define your candidate profile
- ☐ identify position title – amend it if appropriate
- ☐ identify industry sector
- ☐ identify location (currently by zip code in United States)
- ☐ identify associations – college, group, companies
- ☐ construct Boolean string
- ☐ search first on LinkedIn before using other databases
- ☐ always choose Advanced Search
- ☐ narrow your search
- ☐ use other search tools in complementary fashion
- ☐ if a placeable candidate does not emerge, notice contacts and peers and devise information/contact/introduction path via peer group

5 LinkedIn for Collaboration and Third Party Splits

One of the most significant aspects of the recruiting industry today is the use of collaboration or splits between participating recruiters. Paul Hawkinson of the Kimberly Organization and the publisher of the most widely read newsletter on recruiting, The Fordyce Letter, estimates that last year some 16 per cent of all recruiting business was done by way of splits. And it seems that interest in this way of doing business is growing.

The opportunity that networks like LinkedIn bring to the table is the ease of identifying and interacting with potential split partners. No longer is a recruiter isolated by the limits of his or her front door. Recruiters are now plugged in, with a virtually unlimited reach, thanks to broadband connections. They are now operating in a worldwide talent marketplace, no longer a regional one, and splits are an ideal method and way to reach out and touch people around the world.

Some recruiters do not do any splits; others do splits exclusively. With 90,000+ recruiters on LinkedIn, there is obvious potential for recruiters who want to develop split opportunities via LinkedIn.

Bret Hollander

"One of the areas that a lot of recruiters like me are always looking for is splits. I did a search on splits. I simply put the word 'splits' in and of course I got a lot of split stock offers. So I refined it and I put in 'splits' and I put in 'staffing' and 'recruiting' and I came up with six firms that are interested in split arrangements. I have already contacted, in the past, five of those firms, although you know, from my perspective I prefer working splits with firms that do similar kinds of work that I do, but it's an excellent example of quickly identifying people who are willing to do the same kind of work you're willing to do.

"At the same time, if I want to do a search and put in words like 'clearance' or 'polygraph' I'll be able to distinguish between people in the industry, i.e. professionals and people who are recruiters that want to recruit in that industry and that I want to align myself with."

There is an element of risk in splits:

- the risk of misunderstanding or disagreement between the parties
- the risk of rewards being disproportionate to effort by one or other party
- the risk of engaging in a split with another recruiter and not getting paid.

These risks help to explain the growth of associations and agencies which function as brokers for split deals, as is often done with multiple listing services used by realtors worldwide. In the recruiting industry, these groups or agencies bring various tools to bear to help match up job orders and candidates for recruiters and to make sure people are paid, although some online services restrict their role to being essentially an information and job posting exchange rather than playing a more active brokering role.

Craig Silverman, whose firm HireAbility has a co-marketing agreement with LinkedIn, spoke about the possibilities and the risks in split opportunities:

Craig Silverman

"When parties are in a similar space, one is often really good with the client while the other is often really good with the candidate. Most recruiters tend to have strength on one side of the desk or the other. In the recruitment business, on the permanent side, people try to work a full desk. So that means they try to get job orders and candidates. But if you talk to any of those people, they're typically much better at one or the other, and they typically like one side much better than the other. We see LinkedIn as a way to help build the other side of the fence and to complement what we do.

"Splits are somewhat of a dangerous business at times if you don't know who you're doing the split with. There's a lot of money involved; there's contracts. There could be fall-offs, et cetera. So when working with a company like HireAbility, agreements are in place and a next level of qualifications and reference checks. And that's similar to you being in the same company almost and that allows a closer relationship with a higher level of trust. We don't have any issues with any of our splits."

Craig added that HireAbility is really for experienced recruiters, with a minimum five years in the business.

Many recruiters are using LinkedIn to facilitate collaboration and splits directly. It is fair to assume that, for the average recruiter member, being able to find split opportunities could be the second most attractive feature of LinkedIn, after the ability to search for candidates.

Josh Arnold

"LinkedIn is one tool that I use to build networks for splits. There are other tools. I belong to a number of formal and informal networks, not the organized networks where they do splits through a corporate setting. Some are just informal things like newsgroups.

"I write and introduce myself. I say, 'Hi, I'm Josh Arnold from Arnold Career Services and I want to share with you one of the tools that I use that's of tremendous value, the LinkedIn network. As you load in your information, your profile, you are going to be instantly linked to people. This could be a source for you and for people you're linked with from former positions you've had in the professional world. It could be your college, it could be your military service, or it could be your interests. But you're going to link up with people.' And since networking is such a strong component of how we do business in a global economy, this is a win-win for everybody."

Jon Williamson is moving into a stage of looking actively for split partnerships, by developing an informal network of domestic and international recruiters. Right now, very little of Jon's business is through splits, but that is about to change. In his explanation below he illustrates the point made above by Craig Silverman: that most recruiters have a strength on one side of the placement equation and prefer to work in their area of strength.

Jon Williamson

"When I get back into it I expect at least 75 per cent of my business to be splits, because I'd rather put the time into developing a relationship with someone who likes business development and lets me work to provide the candidates and we're both doing what makes us happy.

"I'm in the process of putting my LinkedIn connections into email groups and I'm trying to get to know these people.

"I think the biggest mistake people are making with LinkedIn as a recruiter - I know because I made the same mistake - is they're treating it like a résumé database. It is not a résumé database but profiles of users, individuals who are interested in working with other individuals. Well, maybe 60 per cent - the other 40 per cent are people who have one or two connections and you cannot find them."

A Key Element of Collaboration and Splits is Building Trust and Rapport

Josh Arnold

"One of the things I've been trying to do is to bring more and more recruiters into the LinkedIn network. I do that from the perspective of sharing what LinkedIn offers me, by way of an invitation. So I'm going to reach out to recruiters - and when I say recruiters I really mean independents, people who do it not from a corporation's standpoint but like you and I do. I say, 'These are some of the tools that I use as a recruiter that help me along the way'.

"I will also send that, or a similar message, out to client companies and say, 'I may not have your business right now. You may not be in a position to use agencies. But here's an effective tool that you can use to draw on talent.' And I find that that good deed is a foot in the door."

A Challenge for LinkedIn

According to Scott Allen of the About.com Entrepreneurs Guide and co-author of *The Virtual Handshake*: *Opening Doors and Closing Deals Online*, splits are a big issue for LinkedIn:

Scott Allen, About.com Entrepreneurs Guide and *co-author* of The Virtual Handshake

"With so many recruiters on LinkedIn, and recruiters knowing each other through whatever channels - there are certainly recruiters connected to other recruiters - but even, let's say, if someone is three degrees away and you have a direct contact, and their next contact is a recruiter, and that recruiter's next contact is the person at the end, LinkedIn's premise is built entirely on openness. LinkedIn is built on the idea that anyone is willing to pass leads through for anyone else. The recruiter's business model is built around making money by brokering relationships. That's fundamentally what a recruiter gets paid for, to broker a relationship.

"So that's a conflict of interest between someone who has a need and making connections through various people who know each other to someone who can fill that need. There's a conflict of interest for a recruiter along the line to pass the connection request through to the person they know, especially if the person they know is a client.

"One of the biggest things LinkedIn could do is to figure out a way that would accommodate that and would allow recruiters to continue to monetize that relationship."

Finding Split Partners Through LinkedIn

One of the main advantages of LinkedIn for recruiters interested in collaboration and splits is that the LinkedIn tools facilitate splits by allowing a recruiter to search on some key variables, including the industry area or discipline, focus and geographical location. Having done a search and narrowed the field, the recruiter can then view the others' profiles and get a much better idea of who they are, their areas of specialization, and how they operate. Other information, such as the number of contacts they have and especially the endorsements others may have given them, can help build a picture of what it might be like to do business with them.

It can also be very helpful to see the list of shared connections. This can help to establish whether there is likely to be appropriate synergy.

By the time the recruiter seeks to establish contact, whether through an introduction or by the LinkedIn InMail system, he or she is able to have a quite detailed picture of the person they are interested in collaborating with.

Step-by-Step Illustration of a Search for a Split Partner

Assume you are a recruiter with a U.S.-based software company client that has a branch in the United Kingdom, and they are looking for a Vice President of Sales for that branch.

First, at the Find People page on LinkedIn, construct a search to identify possible split partners as follows.

1. **Industry.** In the Industry box scroll down to "Corporate Services" and then select the sub-category "Staffing and Recruiting." Note that you would use the CTRL key or CMD key (Apple) on your keyboard for multiple selections.

2. **Keywords.** You want to find possible partners who worked with sales executives at the Vice President level in the software industry. In the "Keywords" box type <software ("vp sales" OR "vice president sales")> (without the <> brackets).

3. **Location.** You go to the Location box and select "Located in or near" and then from the scroll-down menu alongside the word "Country" select "United Kingdom." There is no zip or postal code option for countries outside the United States.

4. **Sort method.** Since you are interested in possible collaboration, you will want to know who is endorsing the people the search produces, so for "Sort by" you select "Degrees and endorsers."

There are a couple of other optional boxes to refine the search further, but these details are enough to illustrate the process. The search is now set up to find:

- other staffing and recruiting firms
- in the United Kingdom
- who worked in the software industry
- with Vice President level candidates

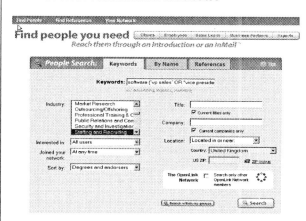

These are the results as on the day of running this test:

As regular users of LinkedIn know, the rest of the results page then provides summaries, with names, of the profiles of the people discovered by the search. You can then click through to get the full profile of each.

Checklist for Action

- ☐ Use LinkedIn's search capabilities to find split partners in the geographical location, industry sector, specialization fields related to your business.
- ☐ Look through each profile, their history and endorsements
- ☐ Evaluate each of the contacts as far as you can in relation to your criteria for a split partner
- ☐ Initiate contact to set up a meeting and verify your potential relationship and working methodology.

6 LinkedIn—a Superior Networking Tool

LinkedIn—More Than a Database

As mentioned previously, recruiters new to LinkedIn usually see it first as an excellent database, where they can find candidates. It is that and more. In fact, LinkedIn was established primarily to be a business networking tool for professionals, enabling members to find the businesspeople they need, through friends and colleagues—people already known and trusted.

As Vincent Wright says, "It's a product to help us do business." Vincent likens the connections made through LinkedIn to being introduced to someone by a friend, as compared to someone coming to your office without any evident connection to you. "If as a recruiter I find someone," he observes "I'm more likely to start a relationship if I'm introduced."

And Shally Steckerl comments:

Shally Steckerl

"I would actually disagree that the primary thing with LinkedIn is to find candidates. That's not really the strength of the network. Networking, whether you do it via e-mail, in person or going to conferences or social events, is not really the art of finding the person that you want to recruit. Networking is getting the word out about what you do and building trust in relationships. So to me, the biggest value that LinkedIn has is as a conduit for me to be able to build trust in relationships."

LinkedIn enables Shally to demonstrate that he is highly connected and "associated with the people everybody else wants to connect with."

LinkedIn provides unprecedented support for the networking requirements of recruiters:

Jerry Bernhart

"I've actually just started using LinkedIn for recruiting. I'm kind of in the early stages, so I can't give you a lot of hard and fast results - just yet. But I'm noticing people are starting to e-mail me, asking me to link into their network. How valuable is that? That's fantastic!"

This is consistent with the recurring message from power user recruiters, that networking, which is what LinkedIn was built for, is not so much about going out and finding people to fill job vacancies, but about building trusted relationships.

Recruiters typically have three key objectives for their LinkedIn networking:

- to help find candidates
- to identify new business possibilities
- to connect with other recruiters

For each of these objectives, recruiters need an extended, high quality network.

Several recruiters made the point that it is neither necessary nor efficient to rely solely on LinkedIn for building and maintaining your network. Shally Steckerl makes the point that even the 3.8 million LinkedIn members he is connected to are still an "insignificant proportion of the global population." He sees LinkedIn as a "magnifier" of his network.

The trust basis on which LinkedIn is built, and the referral system, provides credibility for contacting others.

Al Siano,
Owner and
President,
Business System
Technologies
Corporation

"I see LinkedIn in the context of social networking as a method of building rapport more efficiently with a candidate and with others. In our business you have to rely heavily on the Internet and the telephone, and by getting a referral from someone else you can often improve your ability to have credibility a little bit more rapidly than might be possible by just dialling the phone or sending an e-mail."

A number of recruiters told of using LinkedIn to help others in their network. Susan Hand, Executive and Senior Recruiter at Getronics, told of being able to help a member of her network, a former employer, achieve significant business growth through connections made on LinkedIn.

Susan Hand

"I've created business leads, for myself, departments and contacts. If I see a message or a need I'm happy to connect people with each other. Because of that, the camaraderie that comes with LinkedIn has broadened my network to reach to each of the coasts, plus India and Singapore. I recently saw a need, with a former employer, of business in Brazil and Mexico. I knew that I had some contacts who were experts in that field and I was able to connect the organizations. My former employer has now increased their market share in Brazil and Israel by 20 per cent."

Developing Trust Relationships Virtually

Part of the good business sense, as distinct from altruism, in helping others through networks is that this is an essential part of building the trust on which effective networks rely.

John Zweig,
Senior
Staffing Manager,
Logitech

"LinkedIn has been a referral product for us that's actually successful, almost to the same extent as an employee referral program. Just today I've received three candidates that were referred by LinkedIn members who read a posting. And that's how it's been working consistently over the last five months. The system works. And the system's working because it's a trusted source. People are trusting other people who are networking, on a business kind of level.

"I wrote to the LinkedIn people the other day: I'd just made my twenty first placement, as a result of LinkedIn. I don't use anything else."

Scott Allen spoke of the challenges being faced in the new era of virtual networking for business development:

Scott Allen

"I think that we're still in the early stages of understanding how to build business relationships virtually, how to communicate effectively, and how to build trust and friendships. And all of these things are moving beyond just the mechanical aspects of business communications tools, really understanding the differences of how we build relationships, with these tools being the fundamental form of communication, instead of eye contact and a handshake."

Using the LinkedIn Network To Find A Passive Candidate

Craig Silverman explained how a recruiter can use networking via LinkedIn to surface passive candidates, effortlessly:

Craig Silverman

"There are a lot of people on LinkedIn. They have profiles and networks. They could be sitting at their desks and be very happy in their current positions. Many people are. They go day-to-day and enjoy the people that they work with, their companies, and their jobs. If one of those people happens to be a friend of yours, let's say, and I was to come to you and say 'Hey, Bill, I'd really like to meet your friend Steve. There might be some things we could talk about in the future and potentially partner together,' and you know me and are comfortable with me, you might introduce me to Steve.

"Again, he might not be looking for work today but the fact that he knows me, that now I focus in his marketplace, I might call him for a referral and say 'Steve, I know that you're a specialist in the bio-tech arena and I'm looking for somebody for one of my bio-tech clients and could you maybe introduce me to somebody that you might know that has this type of skill set?' And sometimes a guy like Steve steps up and says, 'You know what, Craig, that sounds like something that I'd be interested in.' And they just made that move, from passive to active. You can do that in a very indirect fashion, without making somebody uncomfortable, and have an opportunity to build a relationship with them."

Networking: A Key to Accessing Difficult-to-Find Candidates and Clients

Networking is extremely important for Ron Bates, whose Stratford Group identifies 80 per cent of its candidate flow coming from networking, the other 20 per cent coming from direct calling and reaching out via e-mail to candidates they have been able to identify. Ron notes that some candidates can only be reached, in practice, through networking:

Ron Bates

"The reason why we rely so heavily on networking is that it's one thing if you're doing the replacement search for Lou Gerstner as CEO of IBM, where there might be thirteen candidates in the world qualified for that role. It's another thing if you're doing a position that reports into that role, let alone a Vice President search for a pre-IPO start-up nobody's ever heard of, where there could be literally thousands of qualified candidates. And the only way to get to a lot of these people is through networking.

"Because there's no way to identify them unless you have the most amazing database in the world, with all the great search capability in it to identify that somebody had a twenty year career at Kodak three jobs ago but the last job they were at, or the present job, wasn't necessarily applicable, so you would never be able to target or identify that person. And how you get to them is through networking, to get to that person."

Jason Lesher,
Senior Recruiter,
CDI Corporation

"Typically people change jobs fifteen times in a lifetime. You need a network of people you can call."

No More Cold-Calling

Because LinkedIn provides access to detailed information about members, through the members' profiles, and is constructed on the basis of trusted connections, recruiters who do not relish the idea of cold-calling enjoy the fact that every contact made through LinkedIn is effectively a warm contact.

Stuart Thompson

"Once I have an idea of what it is we're looking for I start to throw the net out and start to do searches within LinkedIn, to try to find those people we'd like to talk to. Sometimes I know their names already, but it's a matter of getting an easier introduction than a cold call. And that's where I've seen some of the really great value of

LinkedIn is that it's an unobtrusive, easy way to get in front of people without people feeling like they're being harassed.

"And if they don't respond positively to you, because they may not be interested in the job, they previously wouldn't respond to a cold call or something that's very recruiting-intensive, but through LinkedIn they may think 'Well, I'm just building my network and this may come to benefit me down the road'. And they seem much more apt to respond and start the conversation."

Being Findable

The importance of the LinkedIn member's profile came up so often in the interviews that it is worth repeating here in the context of networking. Recruiters wanting to take full advantage of the networking potential of LinkedIn as a networking tool make sure their profiles are complete and up to date.

Several recruiters commented that they also recommend to their candidates that they keep their profiles up to date. Joe Pelayo says: "The most important thing people neglect is their LinkedIn profile."

Case Study: Using the LinkedIn Network to Help a Client With a Challenge

Doug Beabout says LinkedIn is "tremendous" in terms of helping him maintain and build his recruiting business, building on his knowledge of his clients and customers and mutual referrals between them. He gave an example of networking through LinkedIn to help a client with a challenge for which he had not at that point had an assignment:

Doug Beabout

"I had a company that I was working with in the consumer products industry and they were having a great deal of trouble with the conversion of one type of packaging material to another, and they had no idea how to do that. They didn't want to necessarily fill a search assignment at that point or issue one for me to go out and find a solution provider. They were just on the burgeoning point of worrying about this concept, this notion of making money and saving money, and doing many creative things with this new, very new, under-the-radar-screen packaging material.

"By looking through LinkedIn I was able to reach a few people, then in turn reach a few more. Eventually I got a guy was in fact the author of a technical journal on that subject and had hands-on development experience with this new material. And they got to know one another. Which I might add, in turn, ended up bringing them to a proposal for a solution to implement the material, but it brought Doug Beabout a search assignment for a senior packaging development engineer, which I subsequently filled.

"Everybody in that circle was a winner, and I know if LinkedIn had not been available, the likelihood - I can't say it would have been impossible - but the likelihood of us being able to have connected as expediently as we did would have been greatly diminished."

The Power of Groups

As we discussed in Chapter 2, effective networking with LinkedIn requires an understanding of the role of LinkedIn groups.

There are two kinds of LinkedIn groups: the affinity groups officially approved as part of the LinkedIn network, and those which are not formally part of LinkedIn but where LinkedIn members network and exchange information and views.

On the official LinkedIn for Groups level, there is a wide variety of groups, including alumni organizations, conference groups, corporate groups, networking groups, philanthropic non-profits, and professional organizations. These need to be officially approved by LinkedIn.[10]

Other groups are constituted separately from LinkedIn. There are several notable groups such as My LinkedIn Power Forum and LinkedInnovators, seeking to leverage their LinkedIn membership. These are independent of LinkedIn and not affiliated with LinkedIn, but provide forums for exchange of information and often-vigorous discussion about such subjects as how best to utilize LinkedIn and suggestions for improvements to LinkedIn, as well as opportunities for LinkedIn members in specific professional, industry or interest sub-groups to discuss matters of common interest.

---

10. Details about LinkedIn official Groups are available at: https://www.LinkedIn.com/static?key=groups_directory

Several interviewees commented that membership of the discussion-focused groups has been very helpful for their understanding and utilization of LinkedIn:

Beth Banger-Meehan, *HR Sourcing and Recruitment Service Area Manager,* **Providence Health System**

"You get a tremendous amount of information. People are very willing to share all of their experience out of those groups if you are linked in to them. I've found in the past probably six to eight months just a fountain of information that I've been able to use with my staff and myself. And I think the best part about that network, is that someone can ask a question and people respond immediately. You get things that are real-time, things that you can use immediately, research that you can use immediately. I think that's a real plus for those groups."

TIP For Networking Events—Carl Kutsmode finds that membership of LinkedIn provides him with an excellent ice-breaker at networking events and a very efficient means of follow-up after these events:

"You start talking to somebody you are networking with and you say, 'By the way, are you on LinkedIn?' And I'm finding about five to six of every ten people are on LinkedIn. So what I end up doing, I've got into the habit of inviting everybody I meet to my LinkedIn network. And the ones that are already on have really enhanced my network tremendously. I think it goes back to that branding thing. I'm getting the word out much better through those connections than I could do just on my own."

A Core Competency

Peter Weddle

"Networking is a core competency of the best recruiters online, as well as offline. And if you're going to use advanced technology like LinkedIn to facilitate your networking, make sure you use it as an expert would use it and not as someone who's simply trying to build a great big Rolodex™ in the sky."

Ronda Woodcox spoke about the importance of contributing something to the network.

Ronda Woodcox

"Be open and use your network and give something back. I think that as recruiters we're all about what's going on in the immediate moment but I think you have to give something back, and provide expertise, or offer opinions, or be willing to do more than just say, 'Hey, Joe, I have this great position. Let's talk about it!'

"There's a really good analogy that I heard a while ago - it's a bank account and you have to make some deposits into that account before you can make a withdrawal."

Checklist for Action

- ☐ Invite new contacts to join LinkedIn
- ☐ Keep in touch with your network to surface passive candidates
- ☐ Tap your network for hard-to-find candidates
- ☐ Check your profile regularly to ensure you are readily findable
- ☐ Help others in your network connect with one another
- ☐ Expand your membership of groups

7 Conclusion

This chapter provides a quick overview of the points covered in this book and lessons that have emerged. For those who want to put those lessons into action immediately there is a seven-point checklist for action.

Recruiting is a great industry, where a recruiter, in his or her daily work, can have a profound influence on the lives of many people. When making the connection between the client who is looking for the best person for a key position and the candidate looking for a new opportunity, a role that can enable the candidate to perform at his or her best, getting it right makes all the hard work worthwhile.

It has been a great privilege to gain access to the knowledge, experience, "tricks of the trade", success stories and case studies shared so generously by the many experts interviewed.

Sondra Fuller,
Vice President and co-owner,
Pure Bioscience Recruiting, LLC

"I'm beginning to hear of others' success stories. I'm beginning to hear people say, you know, this is just the best tool I've ever had. It really has supplanted just about everything else. I don't use job boards. I very sparingly ever used them before. I've always relied on who did I know or who knew someone whom I knew, et cetera, and networked that way. And LinkedIn is a giant network, just multiplied many times over. It's ideal."

Recruiters are a significant group on LinkedIn and this is fully recognized by LinkedIn's owners and management. In the interviews for this book the opportunity has been taken to solicit comments and suggestions from recruiters about ways in which LinkedIn's already excellent product could be further enhanced and although these comments are not featured in the book they are available on the recorded interviews and have been drawn to the attention of LinkedIn.

Hans Gieskes,
Chief Executive Officer and co-founder,
H3.com

"LinkedIn has built an incredibly useful database. My personal impression is that lately it almost seems easier for people to get into LinkedIn than it was in the past and they have to really watch quality control from that point of view. But I think being able to map networks and find people the way they do is a market that Monster never solved. Monster has from the beginning very diligently built the résumé database, but has always said, and I agreed, that it's only accessible by search professionals and they have to pay for access.

"LinkedIn has built a network by making it available to everybody, in the first instance for free, and now they have started charging recruiters. I think they can charge recruiters anything they like; recruiters will pay. At the end of the day, if you think that's where you can find the right talent, you will pay and it will still be a pittance compared to the fees that you can earn with those candidates."

Overview

1. Technology, especially the Internet/World Wide Web, has:

   - changed forever the way the recruiting business is done
   - extended the recruiter's reach
   - increased the speed of the process
   - opened up access to organized information about candidates, companies and competitors
   - provided new tools for business development and business continuity
   - opened a new era for splits and other direct, unbrokered collaboration between recruiters

2. The basics of the business remain and are only enhanced, not replaced, by technology.

   Recruiting is still at core a people business and no technology can replace the need to work directly and effectively with people in:

   - finding candidates
   - finding businesses with positions to be filled
   - establishing and building trusted relationships
   - managing and steering the process of helping a company, made up of specific real people
   - deciding that an individual person whom you have presented is a great fit for the position
   - building relationships with clients who are happy to pay you for your work, and who know that they and your candidate will still be happy with their choices months and even years later and will recommend you to others
   - finding and building trust relationships and collaborations with other recruiters to achieve win-win business.

Ronni Marks,
Director of Human Resources,
The Peak Organization

"A person I know works in the technology field. She shared with me that she has made a placement because she was specifically able to put in the LinkedIn search the technology skillset that was needed, and it's working really well for her."

Key Lessons

1. LinkedIn is an excellent online tool for recruiters, for
    -   finding candidates
    -   finding business
    -   getting endorsements from clients and colleagues –even competitors!
    -   getting introduced
    -   third party splits
    -   marketing yourself
    -   networking

2. The premium Business and Pro accounts offer far more accessibility to the network than the free Personal account

3. LinkedIn for Groups and other LinkedIn-related groups are an excellent networking resource

4. LinkedIn is a must-use database for seeking candidates in top-paying executive and technical specialist roles

5. Recruiters working in the "mid-range", with positions paying $50,000 to 100,000, need to work on adding value to their services, recognizing that in-house Human Resources people in companies can also utilize LinkedIn and other online tools and by-pass external recruiters

6. Savvy recruiter users of LinkedIn realize that:
    - it is not just a database but a highly organized one with unique search features, providing access to information not readily available publicly elsewhere
    - it is also, and much more, a superb marketing tool
    - it is a trust-based network

7. Many users simply do not realize what powerful tools exist "under the hood," waiting to be used

8. LinkedIn is a powerful resource for recruiters to enable their candidates to present themselves at their best—coaching them with their profiles, endorsements, network building—and to maintain a trust relationship with a range of potential candidates for future positions.

Donato Diorio,
Founder and Chief Executive Officer,
BroadLook Technologies

"I've got some very specific rules on leveraging LinkedIn. Number one is I tell it to everybody. Whether I can help somebody or not, if somebody can buy our product and make use of it, great. Not everybody can. But I still have a connection out there and if they're a good connection I tell them 'Hey, there's this great tool called LinkedIn! Let me tell you about it.'

"Where I personally use LinkedIn is this: we all get to the end of a sales cycle and people ask for references. And I like to tell people the reality is anybody can provide a reference. Anybody can have one person out there that they can use time after time that's going to say 'Bill is great' or 'Donato is great' or something along those lines. I would prefer to give them an open access to my network and say: 'Here's thirty public testimonials, from Fortune 10 companies down to a mom-and-pop shop. Feel free to call any of them.' It's a much stronger reference."

Checklist for Action

☐ Work on your profile – build it out, make it a true marketing tool (hint: study what the high volume-billing recruiters interviewed for this book have done with their profiles!)

☐ Connect, connect, connect – make LinkedIn the valuable marketing tool it can be for you by making and maintaining great connections

☐ Give and get endorsements

☐ Join and participate in LinkedIn groups – on LinkedIn itself and other LinkedIn related groups

☐ Consider upgrading to a premium account – Business, Business Plus or Pro – to gain greater reach and efficiency within the LinkedIn network

☐ Increase your efficiency in sourcing candidates by advertising on LinkedIn Jobs

☐ Remember it still is and always will be a people to people business

☐ Use LinkedIn to build your position in the profession, learn from others and establish peer-support networks and business-enhancing relationships with other recruiters and companies.

Bill Vick

"I've been blessed with the opportunity of interfacing and talking with leaders in the employment industry. The process has re-shaped my view of how I network personally and how I think recruiters could network to increase their productivity.

"As an example, before conducting these interviews, my view of LinkedIn was somewhat myopic. I only saw it as a candidate database. After talking to experts in the field, I realize it's much broader, much more flexible and almost a recruiting platform for success. My recommendation for anybody who is serious about their business and the bottom line is to get involved with LinkedIn today, not tomorrow."

appendix

A References and Resources

LinkedIn Selected Links

- **Advanced Search**
  https://www.LinkedIn.com/search

- **Business Account**
  https://www.LinkedIn.com/static?key=business_info_more

- **Find People**
  http://www.LinkedIn.com/ns

- **LinkedIn official groups** are available at
  https://www.LinkedIn.com/static?key=groups_directory

- **Search by Keywords**
  https://www.LinkedIn.com/static?key=pop_more_search#
  srchkey

- **Search by Name**
  https://www.LinkedIn.com/static?key=pop_more_search#
  srchname

- **Search for References**
  https://www.LinkedIn.com/static?key=pop_more_search
  #srchref

- **Search – main page**
  https://www.LinkedIn.com/search

- **Special Search Types**
  https://www.LinkedIn.com/static?key=pop_more_search
  #stypes

Select List of Unofficial Groups on LinkedIn topics

- **My LinkedIn Power Forum**
  http://finance.groups.yahoo.com/group/MyLinkedinPower Forum/

- **LinkedInnnovators**
  http://finance.groups.yahoo.com/group/LinkedInnovators/

- **The DallasBule Business Network**
  http://www.dallasblue.com
  and follow the links to LinkedIn related services

- **LinkedIn Bloggers**
  http://finance.groups.yahoo.com/group/LinkedinBloggers

- **LICM** - for users of the LinkedIn Contact Management System, developed by Arnnei Speiser at Mega AS Consulting Ltd and offered as Freeware
  http://groups.yahoo.com/group/LICM/

B People and Their LinkedIn Profile Links

David Allen | President, Century Associates, 35 year veteran in recruiting, with over 20 years experience in Executive Search for the Information Technology field
LinkedIn Profile:
https://www.linkedin.com/e/fpf/51287

Scott Allen | About.com, Entrepreneurs Guide, Co-author of "*The Virtual Handshake: Opening Doors and Closing Deals Online*"
LinkedIn Profile:
https://www.linkedin.com/e/fpf/2369

Brian Anderson | President, BA Search Group Executive Search Consultant
LinkedIn Profile:
https://www.linkedin.com/e/fpf/762009

Josh Arnold | Owner, Arnold Career Services A nationwide Recruiting Service
LinkedIn Profile:
https://www.linkedin.com/e/fpf/966156

Beth Banger-Meehan | HR Sourcing and Recruitment Service Area Manager at Providence Health System
LinkedIn Profile:
https://www.linkedin.com/e/fpf/141450

Ron Bates	Managing Principal, Executive Advantage Group Inc., & No 1 linked person on LinkedIn **LinkedIn Profile:** https://www.LinkedIn.com/e/fpf/141450
Doug Beabout	Professional Speaker, Training & Coaching Consultant and Contractor **LinkedIn Profile:** https://www.linkedin.com/e/fpf/48248
Jerry Bernhart	Owner, Bernhart Associates Executive Search **LinkedIn Profile:** https://www.linkedin.com/e/fpf/438998
Randy Bogue	Managing Director, Venator Partners **LinkedIn Profile:** https://www.linkedin.com/e/fpf/283977
Tina Boone	Recruitment Director, S. J. Gallina & Co. **LinkedIn Profile:** https://www.linkedin.com/e/fpf/570405
Greg Buechler	Director of Talent Acquisition at iHire, Inc. **LinkedIn Profile:** https://www.linkedin.com/e/fpf/181715/
Gerry Crispin	Co-founder CareerXroads **LinkedIn Profile:** https://www.LinkedIn.com/e/fpf/44779
Donato Diorio	Founder & CEO BroadLook Technologies **LinkedIn Profile:** https://www.linkedin.com/e/fpf/24085

Marc Freedman	CEO RazorPop, Founder and Executive Director at LinkedinPro[11] and LinkedIn University, and Executive Director, DallasBlue Business Network **LinkedIn Profile:** https://www.linkedin.com/e/fpf/25415
Chris Forman	CEO, AIRS **LinkedIn Profile:** https://www.linkedin.com/e/fpf/31238
Sondra Fuller	Vice President at Pure Bioscience Recruiting LLC. Co-Owner **LinkedIn Profile:** https://www.linkedin.com/e/fpf/520502
Konstantin Guericke	VP Marketing and Co-Founder at LinkedIn **LinkedIn Profile:** https://www.linkedin.com/e/fpf/1244
Hans Gieskes	CEO / Co-Founder at H3.com **LinkedIn Profile:** https://www.linkedin.com/e/fpf/360315
Glenn Gutmacher	Recruiting Researcher at Microsoft, Founder Recruiting-online.com **LinkedIn Profile:** https://www.linkedin.com/e/fpf/776667
Keith Halperin	Recruiting Lead, Senior Recruiter, Recruiting Strategist, Recruitment Process Outsourcing (RPO) Consultant **LinkedIn Profile:** https://www.linkedin.com/e/fpf/651750

---

11. LinkedIn Pro, LinkedIn U, LinkedInDaddy, and similar Dallas-Blue services and web sites are independent resources for users of the LinkedIn networking service, and are not affiliated with or endorsed by LinkedIn

Susan Hand	Executive and Senior Recruiter at Getronics **LinkedIn Profile:** https://www.LinkedIn.com/e/fpf/95328
Taj Haslani	Owner/President NetPixel Inc. **LinkedIn Profile:** https://www.linkedin.com/e/fpf/182667
Bret Hollander	Contingency/Contract Recruiter who specializes in professionals with high-level U.S. Government clearances **LinkedIn Profile:** https://www.linkedin.com/e/fpf/859144
Carmen Hudson	Staffing Manager, North America Business Unit at Starbucks Coffee Company **LinkedIn Profile:** https://www.linkedin.com/e/fpf/246398
Roger King	CEO, Chief People Officer **LinkedIn Profile:** https://www.linkedin.com/e/fpf/50763
Carl Kutsmode	Human Capital Management Consultant - Expertise in Recruitment Process Optimization and Outsourcing **LinkedIn Profile:** https://www.linkedin.com/e/fpf/384312
Jason Lesher	Senior Recruiter at CDI Corporation **LinkedIn Profile:** https://www.linkedin.com/e/fpf/3695688
Ronni Marks	Director of Human Resources at The Peak Organization **LinkedIn Profile:** https://www.linkedin.com/e/fpf/4125560

Eric Misch	Business Development Manager at Mankuta | Gallagher **LinkedIn Profile:** https://www.linkedin.com/e/fpf/2245516
Joe Pelayo	CEO Joseph Michaels Inc. **LinkedIn Profile:** https://www.LinkedIn.com/e/fpf/16548
David Perry	Managing Partner at Perry-Martel International Inc. **LinkedIn Profile:** https://www.linkedin.com/e/fpf/113709
Sandy Sanderson	Founding Partner, Meridian Executive Resources **LinkedIn Profile:** https://www.linkedin.com/e/fpf/6012
Maureen Sharib	HR Researcher - Names Sourcer/Sourcing Methods Trainer - Names Generator at techtrak.com **LinkedIn Profile:** https://www.linkedin.com/e/fpf/850198
Rick Shull	Executive Search Consultant **LinkedIn Profile:** https://www.linkedin.com/e/fpf/1952444
Al Siano	Owner, President at Business System Technologies Corporation **LinkedIn Profile:** https://www.linkedin.com/e/fpf/894277
Craig Silverman	Executive Vice President Sales & Marketing @ HireAbility **LinkedIn Profile:** https://www.LinkedIn.com/e/fpf/95328

Shally Steckerl	Lead Internet Researcher, Microsoft Author, Electronic Recruiting 101, the definitive guide to online recruiting **LinkedIn Profile:** https://www.LinkedIn.com/e/fpf/651750
Jim Stroud	Senior Internet Researcher at Microsoft, searchologist and blogger **LinkedIn Profile:** https://www.linkedin.com/e/fpf/45999
Conrad Taylor	President & Past Chairman of the National Association of Personnel Services (NAPS) **LinkedIn Profile:** https://www.linkedin.com/e/fpf/4672624
David Teten	Online Recruiting Specialist, CEO Nitron Advisers, Chairman, Teten Recruiting, Co-Author, The Virtual Handshake: Opening Doors and Closing Deals Online **LinkedIn Profile:** https://www.linkedin.com/e/fpf/1575
Stuart Thompson	Recruiting Manager at Take-Two Interactive Software, Inc. **LinkedIn Profile:** https://www.linkedin.com/e/fpf/1244
Suzanne Tonini	CIO/Sourcer and Research Specialist, Founder at MTR Inc. **LinkedIn Profile:** https://www.linkedin.com/e/fpf/131975
Bill Vick	Senior Partner at Ternosky & Vick Executive Search **LinkedIn Profile:** https://www.linkedin.com/e/fpf/26994

Des Walsh	Business Coach and Blogging Evangelist at deswalsh.com **LinkedIn Profile:** https://www.linkedin.com/e/fpf/1230770
Peter Weddle	Owner WEDDLE's LLC **LinkedIn Profile:** https://www.linkedin.com/e/fpf/3849168
Kevin Wheeler	President/Founder, Global Learning Resources, Inc **LinkedIn Profile:** https://www.linkedin.com/e/fpf/226672
Jon Williamson	Recruiter at Williamson Employment **LinkedIn Profile:** https://www.linkedin.com/e/fpf/570405
Ronda Woodcox	Partner, Talent Scout Recruiting **LinkedIn Profile:** https://www.linkedin.com/e/fpf/521696
Vincent Wright	Founder and President, Wright Enterprises **LinkedIn Profile:** https://www.linkedin.com/e/fpf/264166
Arthur Young	Founder at Delta Resources International & Recruiter.com **LinkedIn Profile:** https://www.linkedin.com/e/fpf/3421229
John Zweig	Sr. Staffing Manager at Logitech **LinkedIn Profile:** https://www.linkedin.com/e/fpf/839360.

Appendix B: People and Their LinkedIn Profile Links

About the Authors, Bill Vick with Des Walsh

Bill Vick (LinkedIn profile: https://www.linkedin.com/e/fpf/26994) spent his early career in executive sales and marketing management with F500 companies focusing on the consumer products industry, computer retail and software industries. He joined Management Recruiters International in 1986 as a recruiter where he was their National Rookie of the year. Subsequent to that, Bill ran his own retained search firm, Vick & Associates which he still maintains.

- In 1991, Bill formed Solo System, which produced software for the staffing industry
- In 1996, he sold his recruiting business and software company to focus exclusively on the Internet where he founded Ad-Cast, a collection of internet companies which included Recruiters OnLine Network (RON), a top 100 site, HR.Net, and TheTalentBank.net
- In 2002, he sold the Ad-Cast collection of companies and launched three not for profit Web sites focusing on recruitment and employment issues: XtremeRecruiting.org, ThePhoenixLink.com, and EmploymentDigest.net

He was a founder and board member of the Pinnacle Society recognizing achievement in the staffing industry, a national speaker for National Association of Personnel Consultants (NAPS), served on the Board of Directors of The Texas Association of Personnel Services (TAPS), was an officer with the Metroplex Association of Personnel Services (MAPS) and a founder of the local Dallas Independent Recruiters Group (IRG). He is an active speaker, and writer on career issues, recruiting trends and employment technology.

Des Walsh (LinkedIn profile: https://www.linkedin.com/e/fpf/1230770) is a business coach and blogging evangelist, with lengthy experience as an executive and consultant in both the public and private sectors. He has authored or co-authored reports and manuals, in diverse fields from government policy in education and the arts, to training manuals for executives in the transport industry.

Des is currently a business coach and specializes in supporting business owners wanting to make effective use of blogging and other social networking tools. He is a founding member of the International Association of Coaches and a member of Coachville.com. A member of several LinkedIn groups, Des is moderator of the LinkedIn Bloggers group.

Ron Bates, *Managing Principal,* **Executive Advantage Group, Inc.** *and #1 most connected person on LinkedIn.*

"LinkedIn is a phenomenal tool for business networkers, job seekers, and recruiters alike. Everyone has different objectives behind the networking they do. Bill Vick's book is a fantastic resource for any recruiter who wants to understand how to get the most out of LinkedIn. The book's value isn't limited to recruiters however. The book is also a great resource for job seekers desiring to maximize their exposure to opportunity by understanding how recruiters utilize LinkedIn to identify great candidates, in addition to having obvious applicability to business networkers in general."

Conrad G. Taylor, *CPC/CTS,* **President, Past** *Chairman,* **NAPS**

"You can be sure that in my role as President of the National Association of Personnel Services (NAPS) I will be recommending our members to get LinkedIn and to read and listen to this book."

David Perry, *Managing Partner* at **Perry-Martel International Inc.,** and *Author* of **Guerrilla Marketing for Job Hunters,** with **Jay Levinson**

"LinkedIn is a great tool! Whenever you start a search, the hardest part is, you know, starting. Where do you find them? Who are the people you need to talk to? LinkedIn is a great tool for primary sourcing. It's a great tool for trying to break into a company to find out who to talk to. Because even if the perfect prospect is not directly in LinkedIn, one of their co-workers probably are."

Craig Silverman, *Executive Vice President,* **HireAbility - The Recruiting Network**

"What I've learned since becoming an avid LinkedIn user is that there are a large amount of recruitment functions and services that it aids. LinkedIn has been a great way for our recruiters, for example, to locate new business opportunities and build relationships with hiring managers that want to take advantage of recruitment services, and at the same time a great way to find candidates that might be passively or actively looking for work."

Shally Steckerl, *Lead Internet Researcher,* **Microsoft, and** *Author,* **Electronic Recruiting 101, the definitive guide to online recruiting**

"There's always going to be information on the Internet that can't be found using search engines. When you look at LinkedIn, you have a highly structured database, or Rolodex®, of information which can be used in a much more organized way. A lot of times the privileges of membership allows you access to information that wouldn't normally be publicly available."

Jerry Bernhart, *Owner,* **Bernhart Associates Executive Search, Member of the Pinnacle Society**

"I've actually just started using LinkedIn for recruiting. I'm kind of in the early stages, so I can't give you a lot of hard and fast results – just yet. But I'm noticing people are starting to email me, asking me to link into their network. How valuable is that? That's fantastic!"

Brice Benefiel,
Sr. Recruiter -
Information
Technology,
Omnikron Systems
Inc.

"It is a great read, I am actually on my second go around."

Vincent Wright,
Moderator, **My**
LinkedIn Power
Forum

"Bill Vick and Desmond Walsh have written a very good book, one that every recruiter using LinkedIn should have. (I also think non-Recruiters may also benefit from insights in 'Happy About LinkedIn for Recruiting'.)

From its inception, I knew that if Bill Vick were to get involved, 'Happy About LinkedIn for Recruiting' would be a successful book project. Bill pulled out all the stops to interview top recruiters and sourcing professionals in the staffing industry to get their take on best practices for Recruiters who are looking to maximize the value of LinkedIn in their daily business lives.

I haven't really added up the numbers for the 7 bonuses that come with the book but, it appears that if an astute Recruiter purchased the book and used all 7 bonuses, they could make at least 10 times the cost of the book from the bonuses, alone. Of course, they could make MANY times that were they to put the book into practice.

Because there are many Recruiters on MLPF and a number of others who might benefit from a close reading of 'Happy About LinkedIn for Recruiting', I'm happy about recommending it to you, your staff, and all members of My LinkedIn Power Forum.

Kudos to Bill and Des for a job well done!"

This book comes with...

a password to a special Website where you can listen to the raw interviews, find additional resources and have access to over $500 of special offers including a **free LinkedIn job posting** (normally $95). Check out the page at the beginning of the book that's titled *"Steps necessary to get access to the additional content and special offers"*.

Printed in the United States
46752LVS00002B/1-126